Praise for *Row for Freedom*

"*Row for Freedom* is an inspiring story of resolute determination and courage, born out of one woman's conviction to tackle the great injustice of human slavery. This story shows us that with perseverance and commitment we each can make a difference to the condition of humanity."

— Rt Hon William Hague MP
Author, *William Wilberforce:
The Life of the Great Anti-
Slave Trade Campaigner*

"Great story—brilliantly told. Inspirational in the best way."

— Sir Matthew Pinsent CBE
Four-time Olympic rowing
gold medalist

"I supported Julia and her crew throughout their rowing campaign, which raised much needed awareness of the scale and effects of human trafficking in the UK and globally. *Row for Freedom* is an inspiring example of bravery and determination. I wish Julia all the continued success."

— Fiona Mactaggart MP
Founder and secretary,
All-Party Parliamentary
Group on Prostitution
and the Global Sex Trade;
and co-chair, All-Party
Parliamentary Group
on Human Trafficking/
Modern-Day Slavery

"The impact of *Row for Freedom* ripples far and wide, inspiring us all that we can play our parts to see the eradication of modern slavery. You cannot be anything but inspired and moved to action after reading Julia's book."

— Kirsty Gallacher
British TV broadcaster
and Sport for Freedom
ambassador

"Some stories are the stuff of legend-making and must be told. They are tales of heroism and duty and relentless determined passion. Julia's story is all of that—it is also the potent pursuit of purpose. This journey in words gives us just an inkling of both the horrors of human trafficking and the grit one woman has to stand up and state her anger at the peddlers of injustice, with a cry for freedom and a row that stretches even the most insistent to adoration and respect. The fact that nations now are alert to this ugly money-grabbing system of trading human lives, and governments are acting to reverse the tide again, is in some major part a tribute to this woman and to her agony for freedom—for her and for the captives, it is just beautiful."

— Lord Hastings of
Scarisbrick CBE, PhD
Parliament, United
Kingdom

"The physical achievement in crossing the Atlantic, breaking records along the way, is more than matched by their achievement in raising awareness of an issue that is closest to my heart."

— Catherine Bearder MEP
South East England

"Julia Immonen is an inspiration to anyone who wants to make a difference in this world. She is visionary, brave—and huge fun as well. She is spurred on to achieve her extraordinary feats on sea and land by a single-minded determination to play her part in ending the evil of human trafficking. We admire her more than we can say and commend her book to you."

— Nicky and Pippa Gumbel
Holy Trinity Brompton,
Britain

"I spoke to Julia when she was buried deep in the waves of the mid Atlantic. I heard the pain and the struggle in her voice but also her tenacious, relentless determination for freedom. She is an example of what can happen when you say yes to step out beyond the ordinary."

— Christine Caine
A21 campaign founder
and Equip & Empower
Ministries director

"If you're gonna risk it all, you might as well make it count. Julia Immonen's *Row for Freedom* is a gritty and gutsy adventure, one filled with terrifying challenges and surreal rewards, like the reward of knowing that each relentless pull of the oars as they crossed perilous waters was breaking chains that held others captive. They rowed so others could live free.

"Julia radiates stunning hope and beautiful compassion, both of which drench these pages with a sense that you, too, have an adventure to live and a story to tell. You don't have to cross an ocean, but you do have to face your fears and realize that you can do more than you have ever imagined."

— Louie Giglio
Speaker, author, and
pastor, Passion City
Church and Passion
Conferences

"Passion is often defined as 'the degree of difficulty we're willing to endure to achieve our goal.' That being the case, the story of Julia's Atlantic row is a most remarkable display of passion. With her goal in mind of helping those chained by the shackles of human trafficking and modern-day slavery, she never gives up on hope and never gives in to her fears. The perseverance shown on these pages will inspire you to face oceans of adventure or adversity in your own life."

— Matt Redman
Songwriter; and Beth
Redman, author and A21
campaign ambassador

"Julia Immonen is a hero! This brave and stunning woman has shown us that every ordinary life can bring about remarkable change. *Row for Freedom* will encourage you to believe that every day of your life is pregnant with hope, strength, and the ability to impact our world."

— Lisa Bevere
Messenger International,
best-selling author, and
minister

"A gripping account of how an ordinary woman went on an extraordinary venture to highlight an appalling evil. Honest, authentic and utterly challenging."

— J.John (Reverend Canon)
Speaker; author; and
director, Philo Trust,
England

ROW FOR FREEDOM

ROW FOR FREEDOM

Crossing an Ocean in Search of Hope

Julia Immonen

with Craig Borlase

W PUBLISHING GROUP

AN IMPRINT OF THOMAS NELSON

Published in Nashville, Tennessee, by W Publishing Group, an imprint of Thomas Nelson.

Published in association with D. C. Jacobson & Associates, an Author Management Company, www.dcjacobson.com.

Thomas Nelson titles may be purchased in bulk for educational, business, fund-raising, or sales promotional use. For information, please e-mail SpecialMarkets@ThomasNelson.com.

This is a work of nonfiction. The events and experiences detailed herein are all true and have been faithfully rendered as I have remembered them, to the best of my ability. Some names and identities have been changed in order to protect the privacy of certain individuals involved.

Though conversations come from my keen recollection of them, they are not written to represent word-for-word documentation; rather, I have retold them in a way that evokes the real feeling and meaning of what was said, in keeping with the true essence of the mood and spirit of the event.

Scripture quotations marked NKJV are taken from the New King James Version®. © 1982 by Thomas Nelson, Inc. Used by permission. All rights reserved.

Scripture quotations marked NIV are taken from the Holy Bible, New International Version®, NIV®. © 1973, 1978, 1984 by Biblica, Inc.™ Used by permission of Zondervan. All rights reserved worldwide.

Photo insert: © Guy Bell, www.gbphotos.com. © Brian Finke. © Deborah Paul. © Photographs by Stuart Tipplestun of Barbados Photography, www.Barbados-Photography.com. All photos used by permission.

Library of Congress Cataloging-in-Publication Data is available upon request:

LCCN 2014902293

ISBN: 9780529101471

Printed in the United States of America

14 15 16 17 18 RRD 5 4 3 2 1

Contents

CONTENTS

Foreword

All of us have adventure in the blood. Go back far enough into your family history and you'll find the stories. An ancestor who left his homeland in search of a better life. A distant relative who fought against impossible odds and won. A family who took a risk and made a change.

That's what adventure is. It's about starting the search when we don't know exactly what we'll find. It's about doing whatever it takes to make a change. It's about saying yes to the struggle.

And it's part of all of us.

The question is, how big an adventure is each of us going to live?

I've met a lot of people who have chosen to live their adventures as big as they possibly can. Some of them you know already; others you'll never hear of. But all of them have made that same choice—to jump into the unknown for the sake of something bigger.

I first met Julia as she was about to make that leap. I listened as she talked about rowing the Atlantic.

She was passionate and excited, and she didn't really know what was waiting for her out there on the ocean. She had no idea how tough it would get. But she was prepared to risk it all to make a difference.

She had that look in her eyes. It told me she was ready.

I watched as the row started to unfold. I heard about things that went wrong out there on the ocean, but I knew that we were only hearing a small part of the story.

When you're in the middle of the adventure, you just have to live it. When you're on an expedition, you put your head down and battle through. Storytelling happens after the finish line.

But now that time has come. A couple of years after landing in Barbados, Julia can tell her story. The full story.

Row for Freedom explains what it was really like for Julia and the others as they spent forty-five days hauling themselves across the Atlantic. It details the equipment failures and the emotional struggles. It explores the battles against time, weather, and exhaustion to make it across and break two Guinness World Records. It invites us on board and lets us feel the wind and waves for ourselves.

But it also tells us more. It explains what life was like for Julia in the years and months before the row. It describes the fears and the struggles as family life was thrown into chaos. Knowing what she went through makes her adventure even more remarkable.

And *Row for Freedom* tells us why she did it all. It explains the passion that drives Julia—the unapologetic hope of changing the world. It shows us exactly how this ordinary girl from a London suburb became so passionate about a cause that she'd attempt something like this. It shows us what it's like to wake up to the nightmare of modern-day slavery and realize that silence is not an option.

I know what it's like to chase a dream—and what it's like to encounter fear in the process. Julia's story tells it how it really is. She holds nothing back.

Even though they called it the Row for Freedom, there were plenty of times when their journey felt the very opposite of liberty. It was tough and demanding. It was painful and relentless. It was frightening and dangerous.

It was like all the best expeditions.

Row for Freedom is a great story of a great adventure. It's got all the best ingredients: struggles, setbacks, unforeseen changes, determined faith, plenty of risk, and—right at the very center of it all—a belief that this kind of thing is precisely what you and I were made for.

Bear Grylls

Author's Note: Why Write This Book?

My bookshelf is only half-full at home. I'm not a big reader. So why write a book? Good question. To answer it I need to tell you a bit about myself. I've always thought of myself as a natural-born optimist, a semipro dreamer of big dreams, but even as a child I knew that things often don't turn out quite as well in real life as they do in your head. Even though somewhere within me I had a hunch that something great could happen, I learned to limit my choices, to water down the dreams. Great exam grades; a beautiful house; a perfectly happy, successful, and normal-looking family were beyond my reach.

And then I saw a movie and got stirred up. It was as if someone pulled back the curtain on the real world and showed me the ugly truth that bad things happen to innocent people. For the first time I realized how odd it was to complain about my life not going according to plan. I had my freedom, and I had hope. What was there to complain about?

The revelations didn't stop there. I worked out that nobody's qualified to change the world. No one is clever enough, kind enough, patient enough, or whatever enough to solve the world's problems on his or her own. And those failings shouldn't hold us back.

I changed. I went from self-medicating with relationships and handbags to breaking two world records for ocean rowing. There were plenty of reasons not to do it: I was in debt, I was worried about my family, and a year and a half earlier I'd never sat in a rowing boat. But those reasons weren't big enough to put me off.

Getting stirred up by a cause, rowing the ocean, starting a charity—these things were completely out of character for me. I'm an ordinary girl, but this extraordinary adventure taught me that all of us have the potential to become passionate about some of the things that need changing in this world and work to bring about change.

Along the way there are struggles and difficulties, dangers and setbacks. Yet the things that try to force us to turn around are weak compared to the tiny grain of self-belief that it takes to get out there and try. We need to forget about what we *can't* do and think about what we *can* do.

When I was rowing the Atlantic, my crew and I raced the ocean against a boat called *Dream It. Do It.* I wish I'd thought of that name for our boat. No matter where we're from or what our past has been, we can learn how to dream and act if we overcome whatever version it is of fear that plagues us. I decided to row an ocean because life gets so much better when we stop listening to the reasons why we can't do something. And that's why I decided to write this book.

I wanted to share the story of the row, but there is more than one journey in this book. Yes, there is the one with the waves and the broken equipment and the fire and the exhaustion, but there's another adventure to tell. It's the one where I learned how to listen to my inner optimist and stop allowing fear to limit my horizon. It's the voyage back to dreaming and doing. It's the story of waking up to life.

I hope it helps.

Julia

Prologue: Fear and Fire

I wake to the sensation of being shaken, but I'm alone in this tiny cabin. Almost immediately it happens again, the great shove from the left pushing me violently against the thin sheets of foam that barely disguise the hard walls of the boat beyond it. In seas this ferocious, beneath waves this huge, I could easily end up breaking some bones. I brace myself, my hands and feet stretched out against the walls, holding back the force of the ocean. It's ridiculous that I think I can take on these waters. Like the other four girls on this boat, I'm here only because the ocean allows it.

I close my eyes and picture the scene outside. The only light on the boat is the feebly shining navigation light on the bow. All around us are waves hidden by darkness until the moment they strike. Judging by the way this cabin moves, some of these beasts must be thirty, forty feet high. Sometimes they lift us up before throwing us back down; other times they seem happier to land with their full weight on top of us. Three of my friends are out there on the deck, holding on to their oars, trying desperately to pull against the waters and ride to the top of the waves. They are soaked through and unable to hear each other over the noise of the wind and the waves. At least two of them love every minute of it.

These conditions are tough, possibly the worst yet. Again and again the waves play with the boat, tilting her farther and farther over on her side, every time sending me crashing into the too-thin foam. It's a bad sign, this sideways rolling. It means that we lie parallel to the waves. If a big enough one comes along, it'll send us right over.

"Capsizing is a normal part of ocean rowing," said Simon, our ocean rowing guru. "It's not a matter of *if* you capsize, girls. It's about *when*." We've talked so often about what will happen that I feel as though I know exactly what each of us will do. Whoever's in the bow and stern cabins will work together to rock the boat backward and forward, building up the momentum until the boat flips over. They'll use the handheld radios to let each other know that they're okay, and I guess they'll hope that they won't run out of air before the boat gets righted and that the hatch doors are strong enough to hold back the water. The ones on deck at the time of capsize have to hope that their foot leashes hold fast and keep them tethered to the boat. There's not much more that they can do.

Rehearsing these plans in my head does little to calm my nerves. I'm slammed into the side again. The pushes are harder, and the cabin wall has almost become the floor. Is this what it feels like to be born? I can't believe that we can take this much force and still float, but we do. Just. I desperately want to open the tiny hatch door that is the only way in and out of this space, but I can't. The possibility of a large wave barging its way through the hatch is too great a risk to take. I stay in my cabin that's little larger than a coffin and wait.

When you leave the safety of land behind and row this far into the ocean, you know exactly what it means to fight. Each stroke of the oar is a battle against many enemies, from seasickness and exhaustion to waves as tall as houses and pain that leaves your hands bent in a claw-like grip, making it difficult to let go of the oar. I can handle each of these foes, but fear nearly pulls me under.

The first ocean rower I met was tall, strong, and rugged. He looked like the kind of guy who—if something went wrong with the boat—would be happy tying a rope around his waist, diving in, and swimming the rest of the way, towing the boat behind him. He looked like he could take on any challenge and emerge triumphant. "The thing is, Julia," he said when we first met, "it was the hardest thing I've ever done. I felt constantly exhausted and completely drained. It took everything I had, and even then there were times when I felt unsure that I had what it took to make it. No wonder more people have gone into space or climbed Everest than have rowed an ocean."

That was one of those conversations I wish I couldn't recall with quite so much clarity. That look of pain in his eyes. The way he shivered as he remembered what it had been like. The sigh of relief as he said, "Never again."

Why did I think I could follow his example and be part of a crew that rowed the Atlantic? I'm not like him. I'm not strong, and I'm not the kind of person whose life has been one long string of extreme adventures. I work in TV, love sports, and am a fully signed-up gym bunny who always takes a long shower before stepping onto the street. I have more Louis Vuitton handbags than I know what to do with, and until a little over a year ago, I'd never sat in a rowing boat, let alone tried to conquer waves like these.

Another slap from the left tosses me to the side, and a pile of kits lands on top of me. What am I doing here? I'm trying to change the world. I'm trying to do my bit to end one of the greatest social injustices of the last one hundred years. I'm trying to help innocent people regain their freedom and live without fear. I'm here for Alejandra, the girl whose eyes I looked into as she told me how she had been sold into prostitution. I'm here because I promised I'd cross the ocean for her.

So, you see, failing is not an option. Even if I could persuade the other girls to give up right now—and that would never happen—I'd never be able to live with myself. I'd have let Alejandra down, and I will not do that.

For the first time in many minutes, I can hear something other than the slap of water on the boat or the raging whispers of the wind around us. Really loud shouts come from the deck. I decide to risk it and open the hatch.

The moment I edge open the door and put my head outside, a load of spray attacks my face like a swarm of bees. The three girls are not on their rowing seats, sliding back and forth as they haul us in the direction of Barbados; they are crowded at the far end, peering into the other cabin.

"What's going on?" I shout. "What's the problem?"

"It's on fire!" screams Debs, her eyes wide as she turns to face me. "The watermaker is on fire!"

PART 1

BEGINNING

CHAPTER 1

Childhood

When I was six years old and it was minus twenty degrees Celsius outside, getting dressed was an epic adventure. We started with the thermals—top and bottom—two sets each. They were never very pretty, and I wanted a pink set, but Mum said that it didn't matter since nobody was going to see them. Still, I wanted something nicer than the off-whites that Joy, my older sister, and I wore day in and day out.

Next came two pairs of socks. Add a wooly jumper and pants. Then two pairs of mittens, a cowl, and a hat, and we were almost ready to go. Just needed the snow trousers, warm coat with hood over the hat, and boots. After fifteen minutes we were finally ready for one of us to say the words that made my amazingly patient mother's smile grow even larger: *"Tarvitsen vessan."*

"Really, darlin'?" she replied in her soft Scottish lilt. "You're sure you need the bathroom?"

And so began the ritual of undressing and then dressing again either one of us. Or maybe both. Life in Finland was never fast, especially in the winter. We had to go slow and steady, making sure that we were prepared whenever we stepped out of the house. And my mother was always extra careful with two small girls.

I was born in Jyväskylä, a small city in the middle of the country. It's cold there, but nothing compared to the weather farther north, which is where we moved when I was three. It was there, in Lapland, on the Arctic Circle in the magical city where Santa Claus lived, that my mother learned how to dress us to survive the elements lying in wait outside the door.

When she dressed me, I let my body go floppy and gave in to her hands as they put limbs into sleeves and added layer upon layer of warming fabric to my skin. Mum was always patient, kind, tender, and loving with us. She seemed to have all the time in the world for us, and when she challenged Joy and me to see who could get dressed faster, we never felt as though we were being hurried along to make her life easier. She was just trying to show that even something boring like getting dressed could be fun. It was a simple lesson to learn, but one I've never forgotten.

Those times when my hands flew into a frenzy in an attempt to transfer my clothes onto my body before Joy could transfer hers left another mark on my character: they nurtured my competitive spirit. Sometimes I won and sometimes I lost, but I'm not sure that the result was always the most important thing. I enjoyed the thrill of trying to be the best I could be. And perhaps that was when I began to learn that if I pushed myself a bit, I could do more than I imagined.

Finland was not my mother's home. She was born in Scotland but signed up for a new life when she met and fell in love with my father, a man born and bred in Finland. Within eighteen months of meeting him she had seen every area of her life change—country, language, culture, and climate—all so that

4

she could join the man she pledged to spend the rest of her life with, for better or for worse.

She was used to change. As a younger, single woman, she left the west coast of Scotland and traveled a lot, living and working in both Canada and Pakistan before meeting my dad and moving to Finland. Yet moving up north meant more than a change in climate. We moved from a city with a university, an airport, a railway, and roads with proper sidewalks to Rovaniemi, a town of a few thousand people, some basic stores, a church, and not much else.

It was a simple life. When summer came around and the temperatures rose enough for the snow to melt, we played outside constantly. For months it seemed that the sun never set, giving us endless opportunities to pursue our adventures. Dad played with us in the backyard, and we learned to skate and ski long before we rode bikes. We made snow angels and stared in silent awe as the low sun glistened on the snow. We had no money, yet the outdoors entertained Joy and me free of charge. I always felt a little sad when fall began and the sun began its retreat; for just a few hours each day we'd see it struggling to show itself under the weight of all the night that sat in the sky. When winter won out, the sun vanished entirely, and the night lasted the season. Outside would become dangerous once more.

It couldn't have been an easy life for my mother, being far away from her home and family, learning how to survive the cold, and working out her place in the community. She faced more than her fair share of struggles, but the toughest one was living with my father.

My father was a preacher. He moved around a little, starting out by working with young people and gradually moving up the ladder to run his own church in Rovaniemi. Some people might have turned up their noses at the idea of working for a church above the Arctic Circle on the edge of civilization, but as I remember it, he was never happier than when he was in the church building, pacing up and down the front on a Sunday, speaking of God and the struggles within all of us.

I almost feel as though I have had two fathers: one from my early childhood in the cold and chill of our homeland, then another in my adopted homeland of England. Most of the few memories of my father from our days in Finland are good ones. He was in the yard making bigger snow angels than ours, building epic castles, laughing his big laugh, and smiling his big smile. He doted on us, loved us, and cared for us.

He loved and cared for cars too. Finland has long been the home of motor sport, and my father was a devoted follower. I still remember the way his eyes changed as he got behind the wheel. I liked seeing him happy. It made me smile too.

Although these are most of my early memories of my father, there are others of his anger and shouting. His face would set in stone, his eyes growing cold as the winter moon. Before long, I learned to fear him, to fear his impatience when I couldn't ride my bicycle without training wheels when he thought I should be able to, to fear his frustration when I let him down. He hit me only once. I was fourteen and he caught me hanging out with boys who were smoking, but the damage to our relationship was already done.

If my father's touch sometimes brought danger, my mother's hands brought only gentleness and caring. Her hands tucked us in at night, and her hands smoothed away our hair an hour or so later when she returned to tell us that the noises we heard from the living room were nothing to worry about. We missed her hands when Dad was at the front of the church and we were crouched behind the seats with our coloring crayons and paper, while Mum was sorting things out at home.

It was not until recently that my sister, Joy, and I found out what was really going on. Mum told us how poor we were. The church salary was so small that at one point she took a nine-hour train journey south to beg the church leaders for a little more money. She told us other stories that did not surprise us but made us cry and wish that we could have changed what happened. Those noises at night *were* something to worry about. Our mother remained at home while our father was in the pulpit because she was trying to hide the black eye he had given her the night before. In time none of this surprised us. My later childhood grew accustomed to the rhythm of fists on flesh and china on brick. But I suppose we girls thought that our family was normal. Normal? These days I know there's no such thing.

Finland was a child's paradise. Everything revolved around outdoor living, even when the temperatures crashed low and the weather was wild. Finland was my blonde-haired, blue-eyed home, and I loved it. But when I was six, we left.

I don't remember much about our two-thousand-mile drive to our new home in England. It would have been an epic journey, all of us packed into our bright orange Saab. I do remember that once we had driven the length of the Baltic Sea and passed through more countries than I could count on one hand, England did not feel at all like Finland. There were too many people, not enough open space, and not one single other bright orange Saab to be seen. Finland felt far away.

We settled in the suburb of Slough to the west of London. Even though the Queen's residence, Windsor Castle, is only a few miles away, Slough is the butt of jokes. It is the setting for TV shows that laugh at British mediocrity and the kind of place that regularly appears at the top of lists of the worst places to live in the UK.

None of that would have bothered my parents. They're the least materialistic people I know, and coming from Finland with its lack of a class system, neither of them likely considered that Slough was any worse or better than anywhere else. Proximity to Heathrow Airport was important to them. They wanted to be able to provide hospitality to Finnish missionaries passing through London on their way to or from whatever exotic location their work had taken them. For years our house was full of the excited and the weary, all of them telling their stories. I guess it was exciting. It helped take my mind off what was bothering me.

Even though I was six when we moved, it didn't take me long to work out that we were different from the English. Nobody said anything, but I knew that our house wasn't as nice as other people's, my clothes were not quite the same, and our car was just plain weird. I moved from a country where people liked nothing better than to go outside and enjoy the elements, to a place where the number-one pastime was shopping and doing up the house.

In some ways being different was fine. Many of my new friends were African, West Indian, or Asian, but they knew how to show that they belonged. They wore the right brand of sneaker, ate the right type of lunchtime snack, and got picked up in the right kind of car. I was desperate to belong and powerless to resist. Soon I begged Mum for expensive sneakers and dived onto the floorboard whenever our Saab drove anywhere near my friends.

I used those sneakers well, though. I loved sports, taking part in whatever activities I could. It didn't matter to me what games were being played during lunch break, or whether there were no other girls involved yet; I'd throw myself in, running faster, twisting sooner, and dodging whatever outstretched hands were trying to tag me. And when it came to sports day, I'd be the child taking part in every single event that I could, especially on the track. Sprinting just felt like breathing to me.

As the years passed, money became increasingly important to me. I wanted to be like my friends and go on family vacations to Florida, but we were stuck in a ritual of making annual trips to Finland and Scotland to see relatives and loved ones. Those summers in my homeland were good times, but they didn't stop me from wanting to belong and fit in when I got back to England.

Eventually I stopped inviting people to my house. Whenever someone asked, "What does your father do?" I made his career path sound more glamorous than it was. When Dad spent his days messing around with cars in the garage, I said he was a chauffeur. When he got work as a Finnish translator, I told people that he was in publishing. When he announced that he was going to set up a new business selling water filters, I was ready to say that he was an entrepreneur.

The truth was that Dad was struggling. In Finland he was professionally confident and content, but in England life never seemed to get going for him. His business ventures failed, leaving Mum with massive debts and a garage full of useless water filters. In Finland he was an athlete and a preacher, a man with a reputation and well-known talents. In England he was just another guy with big dreams who never managed to deliver.

I don't think Mum loved England either, but she never had the time to think about it. Once we moved to Slough, she became the primary breadwinner, and she worked hard at her job as a dietitian in addition to caring for me and Joy. When we went to sports clubs, Mum took us. When we ate, Mum cooked the meal. And when the house was in chaos after the latest round of houseguests was off on its next adventure, Mum cleaned up after them.

We weren't poor, but we knew when money was tight. All we had to do was look at our plates. Instead of the usual healthy diet of whole wheat pasta, steak, or steamed fish, we'd tuck into the only meals she could afford: fried eggs, beans, and fries. Mum was the only one who wasn't smiling.

I grew to know the rhythms of my childhood. I liked the way the house felt when it was full of visitors with tall stories and loud voices, and I loved the times when I could participate in sports, especially on the track. I learned to see Mum for the inspiration she was, and Joy and I loved to help out whenever she cleaned house. I liked the way the place looked when it was tidied, dusted, and vacuumed, even though it was never quite as nice a house as I wanted it to be. And most of all, I loved the times when Mum, Joy, and I sat on my bed, the door closed, and talked about anything and everything. In between our giggles we'd hear Dad creaking the floorboards just outside, trying not to make noise but desperately wanting to be allowed to join us. I never let him in.

My earliest memory of Dad's losing it is vivid. It was late December, a few days before Christmas. We were dressed up, headed for a caroling concert at Royal Albert Hall. Our pleasant outing suddenly turned into a nightmare as Dad drove and Mum tried her best to navigate through the London traffic. We must have gotten lost because Dad suddenly shouted at Mum while reaching out and grabbing her by the hair, yanking it down with all his strength. Joy and I were shouting and crying in our seats. Instead of fighting back, Mum turned to us and calmed us down. "It's okay," she said. We quieted down, but we knew it wasn't okay.

Months passed between Dad's outbursts. Life settled into a routine of work and school and clubs and activities and Finnish missionaries sleeping on mattresses on the living room floor. But after Joy and I had gone to bed, we'd hear the sound of a coffee cup breaking against the kitchen tiles. It wasn't all bad. I've met people who experienced far worse. Sometimes I'd hear Dad's volume rise and I'd sprint down the stairs to come to Mum's rescue, but I'd find Mum and Dad laughing. The sense of relief was immense.

So that's me: a girl whose father was a fighter and whose mother was a survivor and who grew up in a village where you would freeze to death if you happened to get stuck outside without proper clothing. I guess my life was always going toward one of two extremes: safety or danger. So far, I've never figured out the appeal of a quiet life.

CHAPTER 2

WAG

I always measured myself against other people, yet I never quite measured up. Our house was too old and too shabby. My grades were too mediocre. My family's status was never quite as good as it could be. Even though I loved sports, I became a teenager who seriously doubted that she could achieve much. So as soon as I was sixteen and it was legally possible, I announced that I was leaving school and doing things differently from the default path that the school was pushing. Instead, I was going to a vocational college to study travel and tourism.

Nice girls like me who went to a nice, high-achieving school didn't leave to study travel and tourism. The commonly held view was that my particular course was reserved for people who had no other options, the ones who couldn't stand the rigors of academic study. According to my teachers, I was embarking on a course you would take if you dreamed of becoming an international business executive but knew you were going to be a waiter or a chambermaid.

There among the trainee hairdressers and future hotel workers I made lots of friends. We learned how to do real jobs that would earn us real money, and I liked the idea of earning a decent wage as Mum did. Besides, they were fun, and I felt that I belonged with them. I'd never been at the top of the class before, but I found that I liked it a lot. And when I first met Ben, things got even better.

Ben was a bit of a legend. His brother competed in athletics at a national level, while Ben was a semipro footballer. He was at college a few days a week, but he didn't need to study. He was on the way to becoming a fully professional footballer. Sometime soon the big money was going to flow for Ben. Everybody knew it.

It wasn't the prospect of money that I liked about Ben, though. He was my first serious boyfriend, the one who was exciting to be around, full of energy and passion. He was charismatic and always the thermostat of any room he was in. Everything about him was different from Dad. Where Dad retreated into his thoughts and appeared to be shrinking with age, Ben was happiness and vibrant potential. Strangely enough, Mum told me that those same qualities attracted her to Dad. When they first met, he was the life of the party, and he made her laugh.

I was naive. I believed Ben when he told me that there were no other girls in his life, even though warning signs were everywhere. He and his friends drove a couple of hours down the freeway for their nights out, and I did not ask why. He became nervous whenever I asked to borrow his phone. More than a few times when I answered it, a girl apologized for having dialed the wrong number. Sometimes we'd be at a club, and other girls would come up and greet him with familiar hugs and kisses. I always felt uncomfortable, but I was so blinded by my love and naivety that I looked away. We were together a whole year before he made it official and told people about me.

Our relationship was nearly perfect. Soon after we got together he turned pro. I'd sit in the stands and feel the emotions rush through me with every kick and tackle. Ben was a striker and scored a lot of goals, and I celebrated every single one of them. Rain, snow, hail, sunshine—nothing stopped me from sitting, standing, and shouting through every match. I learned to love football in the years I was with Ben. All those people sharing the same experience, riding the highs and the lows together. It felt good to belong.

The last match of the season was Ben's last game for the London-based club before he was due to join a new team in a higher league. He was feeling great, like a local hero about to be sent off by his friends and family. I was loving it, too, and went to a shop before the match to pick up a copy of a magazine that had just been published. I stood in the aisle, horrified. There, in black and white among the photos of Ben in action, was a picture of him kissing a girl I had never seen before. I was too angry to go to the match, but when he came to my parents' house after the game, I confronted him. Yet I allowed him to talk his way out of it because I desperately wanted to join him on his next adventure.

Life at home with Mum and Dad changed drastically about the time that Ben and I got together. For the first ten years of our living in Slough, Mum cooked, cleaned, and willingly said yes to any invitation that Dad threw out to the endless supply of Finnish missionaries. Then it stopped abruptly. Mum had nothing left to give, and the house was closed to guests. She'd go to work and come home, exhausted. She gave up cleaning, and Dad gave up inviting people to stay. Both of them started to retreat from life.

So when Ben moved a few hundred miles north, I couldn't wait to follow him. I was twenty-three, and I decided to enroll in a university to study media and PR. My parents weren't happy about my *living in sin,* but I thought that getting a degree would soften the blow. I'm not sure that it did, but they knew my mind was made up.

Our new life was incredible. Ben was earning more money in one month than my Mum did in six, and I loved living in the brand-new, four-bedroom house. After Ben scored with his first touch of the ball in his first match—which happened to be against the team's local rival—a steady flow of kids knocked on the front door, asking for his autograph. I was proud of my home and proud of my man.

Those were the early days of the WAG (Wives and Girlfriends) culture in British football. The WAG has become an increasingly visible part of the game, and the tabloids love to follow their progress as they do what comes naturally: shopping, driving big cars, and pouting at the paparazzi while at matches. Even though I was a student, I wasn't fooling anyone. I was a WAG, too, and proud of it. It was a form of escapism, a chance to dress up and pretend that life was every bit as perfect as I desperately wanted it to be.

Like a true WAG, I drove Ben's oversized Mercedes SUV, maxed out my credit cards, and filled my closet with clothes I barely wore. Even though I was studying at university and had a part-time job in a clothing store, my outgoings were substantially bigger than my income. I spent my student loans on Louis Vuitton handbags.

About a year after we moved in together, we were living separate lives. Eventually I found out Ben was being unfaithful. I felt crushed. Ben and I started going out when I was seventeen, and I put the best years of my life on hold so that I could be with him. I loved so much of our seven years together, but what use were those memories, knowing that he was cheating on me all the time?

I thought I knew what the perfect life looked like, and I thought I was living it. I never had to worry about money, and I never had to worry about people looking down on me for the house

I lived in or the choices I made. But once Ben confessed all, I was finished with him.

Besides, I'd already fallen in love with someone else.

I met him at work. I was going down the back stairs, and he was coming up. Impeccably dressed, Fazil was tall and had a perfect smile. We were just friends at first. He always seemed to be there on the days when I was working, and once he found out I was with Ben, football was an easy topic of conversation.

As we knew each other longer, we talked about our problems as well. Fazil told me more about his background, particularly that his Iranian father resisted the family pressure to accept an arranged marriage and shocked everyone by moving to England and marrying a girl from outside his culture. History was repeating itself; Fazil's father was forcing him into an arranged marriage with a girl in Iran. Unlike his father, Fazil couldn't see a way out, and our friendship deepened as he confided in me. He was scared, angry, and confused.

Between Ben's betrayal and Fazil's arranged marriage, we felt like Romeo and Juliet—two young lovers thrown together against the odds, fighting against the forces that would keep us apart.

So when Ben and I went on holiday to try to patch things up between us, my head and heart were in Iran where Fazil was marrying a girl he'd never met. I was treating Ben the very same way that he treated me, but this betrayal made me feel guilty, and rightly so.

When Ben moved away to join a new football club, he was kind to me. I had another year of study left at university, and he offered to pay my rent on an apartment for the duration. Finally Fazil and I could stop meeting in coffee shops and restaurants and be together.

Fazil and Ben were like two sides of the same coin. They had much in common—fathers who didn't want to know me, a love for good fitted suits, and the ability to make me feel happy—but so much about them was different. Ben was a professional athlete with money and a love for going out with large groups of people. Fazil was a smoker who lived at home with his parents, and his friends were petty criminals and drug dealers. Fazil never touched drugs. In the early days I didn't think their differences bothered me, but in time they did. Especially the drug-dealing friends.

Even though he was a fifty-fifty mix of English and Iranian, Fazil looked and acted as if he were 100 percent Iranian. All his friends were from Iran and Pakistan, and they shared the same outlook on relationships. Many of them had wives in England as well as *personal girls*—white girlfriends. Fazil's wife in Iran was refused a visa to come to the UK (probably due to the letter he and I wrote to the English authorities, begging them not to let her into the country), but it didn't occur to me that I was just another personal girl, someone on the side with whom he could have fun. I was convinced that we were the real deal and that he was seeing no one else. He never wanted to go ahead with the marriage, planned not to consummate it, and intended to divorce her the first chance he got.

Fazil's friends were conservative in their approach to women. They frowned on any woman who was seen in public with a man who wasn't her father, brother, husband, or close relative. Since I had lots of male friends from the university who shared my love of shopping, plus a personalized license plate on my car that made me easy to spot, we had a problem. Fazil wasn't afraid of telling me when he thought I had messed up.

"Julia," he'd say, "I can't have you seen out shopping with another guy. How do you think that makes me look? What do you think my friends think when they see you driving around like that?"

Part of me hated the interrogations. Would a loving or kind guy say such things to his girlfriend? But the louder voice within told me that it was his way of showing that he cared. Surely he wouldn't react this way if he didn't love me so much.

But the matter didn't end there. "What do you think my friends think?" became a regular question between us. I quickly became paranoid about how others perceived me. I had been unfaithful by cheating on Ben with Fazil; perhaps his friends were right. Perhaps I wasn't the nice girl I thought I was.

I stopped going out so much, and because his friends weren't exactly the socializing kind, my entire life started to revolve around him. I retreated from everything but my studies, my part-time job, and Fazil. And while a part of me thought intense love felt like this, I knew I was lying. Although I kept trying to convince myself otherwise, I knew that true love shouldn't be so painful, restrictive, and frightening.

After I graduated university, I moved back down south. I was twenty-six, but still I wanted to be near home, so I rented an apartment that was a ten-minute walk from Mum and Dad. Being close to them was comforting. And after Fazil joined me a month later, I was even happier that I could get home quickly.

By the time we were living in Slough, our verbal arguments had turned physical. We'd moved on from arguing about Ben, but Fazil constantly accused me of cheating on him with people at work. As he yelled, he smashed cups, glasses, and plates, crumpled lamp shades, and slammed doors with the force of a hurricane. One time Fazil grabbed me by the throat and forced me against the wall, while on other occasions he spat on me and ran through a list of harsh names for me. Often clad only in my pajamas, I'd run barefoot out of the apartment and sprint back home to Mum. I did not always run, though; sometimes I fought back with slaps and curses, pushing Fazil aside with all my strength. Once I hit him on the side of his head with his cell phone, and I panicked as he lost his balance and fell to the floor.

As if the violence wasn't enough of a problem, we had serious money troubles. The apartment was just smaller than the amount of my wages. Fazil's job didn't bring in much money, and since he had poor credit, my credit cards got maxed out. Kneeling on the floor of the living room, an ocean of bank statements spread out around me, my face pressed to the floor, I felt desperate. I could see no way out. *Stuff it,* I thought, *let's go on holiday. With debts this big, what difference would another few thousand pounds make?*

When I was with Ben I was sure that I'd be fine if we ever broke up. I could imagine myself living as a single woman. I'd be independent, strong, and free. But now, after two years of being locked into a cycle of unpredictable volatility with Fazil, I wasn't so sure. Could I survive without him? The very idea of living on my own scared me.

About five times our arguments were so explosive that they ended with me packing Fazil's bags and him leaving. Every time, though, as soon as he shut the door and the adrenaline died down, fear took over, and I was desperate to get him back. I had no idea why I felt that way at the time, but looking back I see the truth. I was addicted to the ups and the downs. I came to believe that I wasn't the strong, independent woman that I used to picture in my mind. I was weak and I was wrong and I needed a man like Fazil to hold me together.

Beyond that belief, I was repeating what I'd seen with my

parents. Dad never had grounds to question Mum's loyalty to him, but she carried far more than her fair share of the responsibility for making things work at home. When I was a kid, I often told Mum that she was letting Dad get away with too much, that she was being a doormat. Here I was, doing the same thing and worse. I'd taken on all the debt. I'd soaked up all the fury and handed out plenty of my own.

All the time I was with Ben, I never dreamed of cheating on him. Then, after seven years, my good intentions failed. I regret what I did, and I regret that my actions left me so vulnerable to Fazil's accusations. I regret filling one void with another.

But I'm grateful that I was scared and he was too. I think that fear saved us. Eventually we recognized that if we didn't end our relationship, one of us would end up with more than a few bruises and slap marks. After four years of being together, Fazil left in the heat of our biggest argument.

CHAPTER 3

Broken

Fazil went on a Wednesday, I moved back home on Friday, and on Sunday I was in the car driving to London with Joy so that we could attend church. It wasn't that I particularly wanted to go, but Mum and Dad were out for the day, and the prospect of sitting alone in the house terrified me. For the first time in eleven years I was single. Life felt more fragile than ever, and I had absolutely no idea who I was. I was safe, but I was lost. I was in a fog of uncertainty and fear. Going to church seemed like the least risky thing to do.

That Sunday I sat at the back, feeding on every word spoken from the front. I was desperate, searching for hope and hoping that I would find it in church. Just before the end of the service the vicar—a tall beanpole of a man with a smile like a dentist and a voice like the kindest therapist you've ever met—came to the front, microphone in hand, but said absolutely nothing. The silence grabbed my attention, and I looked up. The vicar stood there, a half smile on his lips, looking around.

Until that point I'd never known that you actually *feel* silence. As I sat, watched, and waited, I felt as though I'd been plunged to the bottom of a swimming pool, where the water pressure starts to make itself known. I looked around, wondering whether anyone else felt it too. For the most part people seemed to be perfectly happy and calm in the waiting. But my heart was pounding, and my breathing felt ridiculously loud. Finally the vicar spoke in a voice as calm and measured as if he were inviting guests to dine with him. He said, "If you feel like giving up, you can come to the front and have someone pray for you."

That was it. No hard selling, no shouting, and no stirring music to get the feet and soul moving. Just an invitation to come to the front of the church. He made no explanation of what would happen when you got there and stated no rules about who could and couldn't come. I felt myself plunged deeper into the pool, my heart rate increasing. Then an invisible finger poked my chest as if to say, "That's you, Julia!" I stood up and made my way to the front as quickly as I could.

The pain was almost indescribable. It seemed as if everything bad that ever happened to me—any pain and sorrow I felt—was sucked into my chest. I had to get it out, or I feared I would suffocate. I stood there, my body doubled over, and I sobbed and I sobbed and I sobbed. My tears were the only way of relieving my pain.

In the following weeks, I felt myself coming apart. I was like an engine that had been stripped down to be cleaned, only I wasn't sure that all the parts were going to be put back together. I started thinking about Ben. Why had I left him? What kind of fool was I to throw away such a perfect life? Then I thought about Fazil, and I felt sickened and ashamed by the violence. How could I have gotten so deep into a relationship that was so destructive? Was he right after all? Was I worth nothing more than constant arguments and a total lack of trust?

And I thought about my father. He made mistakes, but I shut him out so much of the time. He never gloated when I came back to live with them. He just did what he always did: he turned up and loaded the car with all my boxes and drove them home while I confided in Mum. And yet, despite his kindness, I couldn't stop being angry about him.

I sought out a therapist, who helped me see that my relationship with Fazil was totally abnormal; everyone needs to be loved, but what Fazil and I had was not a loving relationship. When, one day, she asked me whether I was ashamed of my house when I was a child, I sobbed uncontrollably. When I finished, we talked about the fact that I always wanted to be normal and that I was looking for it in shopping malls and the perfect-looking house, as if by *appearing* normal, I would actually *be* normal. It didn't occur to me that I should be looking deeper.

Work was a good thing for me in those days. I had started out as a runner for Sky Sports News and was gradually moving up the ladder. Being around athletes was kind of inspiring, and no matter what I was feeling inside, there was always room for a natural high that came from seeing a brilliant goal get scored or watching athletes talk about how good it felt to see all their hard work in training pay off.

Being at home helped as well. I was vulnerable and needed to be someplace safe. Having Mum in the next room was everything that I needed it to be, and her cuddles and kind words worked like healing ointment for my bruised soul. Neither she nor Dad judged me, even though I behaved in ways that went against their religious convictions. They treated me only with patient love and kindness.

After that first visit to church, I wanted to go back, despite the colossal pain and the tears. Weirdly, I wasn't embarrassed by what happened. Maybe your tolerance for embarrassment goes up once you've lost count of the times you've been seen running barefoot down the street in your pajamas, your face marked by tears and red handprints.

At church I felt as though I could be raw and real, which was odd because that wasn't anything like how I remembered the church services of my youth. The old services seemed to be the equivalent of beauty pageants for those with perfect lives—all smiles, success all the way. But not in this new church. The people talked freely about their failings. For the first time in my life I could go to church and feel as though I didn't have to lie through my teeth to fit in.

But there were some differences between me and them. I was still sobbing at the front most weeks, while the leaders seemed to have gone a few steps farther than I had. They had optimism about the way life was working out that I—to my surprise—could not share. At the time getting through each day was an accomplishment. I couldn't imagine being able to daydream about future happiness.

I started going to the church in the evenings too. I enrolled in the Alpha Course,[1] where we'd listen to a talk about the big questions of life and what it meant to be a Christian, break into groups, eat a meal, and then discuss it all. Because the church was full of bright young Londoners who didn't drink the religious Kool-Aid, these conversations were honest, raw, and sometimes awkward. Everything was up for discussion. It was unlike anything I'd encountered.

I started to pray again. I couldn't think of the right words to say, so I talked as if God was like the very best version of Dad that I could hope to know. I did it quietly, on my own in my room. Praying felt odd at first, but it helped.

Down at the bottom of my particular chasm I discovered something that is still changing my life: I needed to forgive my father. I was at church at the time. I thought the days of sobbing were behind me as I listened to the preacher speak about the importance of forgiveness. It wasn't a word that I'd used much in my adult life. Who does? But he was clear: if we don't forgive the people who have hurt us, we end up suffering.

It never occurred to me that I should forgive Dad regardless of whether he apologized to me. But as I sat in church and listened to the preacher, I felt the now familiar prod of the invisible finger on my chest, telling me once more that these words were for me.

I got out of my seat and found my usual place at the front. This time I didn't sob; I roared. Forgiving him meant feeling the pain all over again, and the pain was incredible. Everything that had gone wrong between us raged within me.

This moment was perfectly stored in my memory. Months and years later, I'd remember the details: the rust-colored carpet that smelled of newness; the way my tears felt cold as they crawled over my flushed cheeks; the sound of kind voices soothing me with their words. I seemed to be emptied of all my emotions—the happy as well as the sad. All that remained of me was my most raw, vulnerable form. I'd never felt that way before, but I would feel it again. With my body in pain and my soul exhausted from living on not much more than hope and fear, so many times I'd feel every bit as raw and vulnerable out there on the ocean as I did on the carpet. Remembering that night at church helped me push through some of the hardest times on the row. It taught me that weakness is nothing to be afraid of.

That night after church I went home and asked Dad to sit with me in my room and listen to what I had to say. I held his hand as

I spoke the words I'd been rehearsing all the way home in the car: "*Isi*," I said, using the Finnish word for *Daddy*, "I'm so sorry. I shut you out, and I hated you, and I've treated you so badly. Will you forgive me?"

"Of course I will," he said. "It was only natural that you would feel the way you did. Of course I forgive you."

I went to bed that night knowing that something significant had happened. I felt free, unchained, and released. It was as if all those memories of closing the door on him had been changed, the guilt being wiped away with those first four words of his. I exhaled slowly, as if a lifetime of tension was leaking out of my body. I was ready to start living again.

PART 2

WAKING

CHAPTER 4

Deciding to Row an Ocean

From the outside, it looks like an unremarkable scene. We're just two twentysomething girls (well, I'm only just thirty) who have finished a run alongside the River Thames in London. It's June 2010, and it's a perfectly warm, sunny day. We're cooling down and stretching. We're not even talking to each other, just concentrating on getting our breath back and watching the river traffic as the rowers slice up and down the water. Pausing mid-stretch, my roommate Steph pulls out her headphones and motions to me to do the same. "Julia," she says, her face scrunched up in concentration as she stares at the water, "I've been thinking about something. What do you say we row the Atlantic?"

And so, less than two years after I broke up with Fazil and hit my lowest point in life, this is how it all begins. Neither of us has rowed before, and yet the idea of climbing into a boat and hauling ourselves all the way over to the Caribbean seems to be doable. We're young, recently single, and open for adventure. Why wouldn't we do it? Steph's ex-boyfriend rowed the Atlantic, so I guess she's thinking, *If he can do it, why can't I?* It's not a conventional post-breakup therapy, but it has to be better for us than a spa weekend and a family-sized tub of ice cream.

We practically skip as we make our way back home. We talk about how great it will be to do it, how much fun we will have out there on the waves, and how great it will be to reach the other side. It doesn't for one moment occur to me that we might underestimate the scale of the challenge.

And it doesn't occur to me that it's not enough to want to row an ocean just because it's there or because some guy didn't turn out right or because I need direction in life. I'll need something bigger to get me across. For now, childlike excitement and naivety will have to do.

If I could look a little deeper and stop thinking about how I'll probably have a pretty good six-pack by the end of the adventure, I'd see that there's another great reason to motivate me to row across the ocean. I'd see that everything that's been happening in my life over the last two years has been a buildup to this very moment.

It started back in November 2008. It was one of those cold London evenings where staying warm and dry becomes a motivating factor in any plans for an evening, and I was at the movies with a friend. I've never liked films that freak me out, and I would not have gone with her if she told me what we were about to watch. That's why I hid behind her shoulder as the innocent-looking American teenage girls arrived in Paris, took a taxi with a well-meaning stranger, and ended up being taken by Eastern European criminals. Through my fingers I watched as these two girls were sold into forced prostitution, entering a terrifying world behind closed doors. My heart was thrashing around as I watched the younger girl—now drugged and wearing expensive underwear—paraded in front of wealthy men who hid behind blacked-out glass, bidding for the chance to rob her of her virginity.

I couldn't believe what I was watching. Actually I *could* believe it; I just didn't *want* to believe that even though the film was a work of fiction, allegedly it was based on a true story—one that was painfully common. Maybe women are sometimes forced to work as prostitutes, but it is incredibly rare, isn't it?

Leaving the movie theater, I tried to soothe my mind with these thoughts, telling myself that the gap between real life and Hollywood was as wide as ever. But as the days passed I found it impossible to put the film out of my mind. Like a headache that refuses to be calmed by over-the-counter meds, I couldn't ignore it. Part of me knew that the trade in human flesh was more prevalent than I imagined.

What bothered me most was the violation. I'm a trusting person who believes that the world is a good place filled mainly with good people. I've shared taxis with strangers and never paused to think about the potential consequences. But this film showed me a different story of the violation of an innocent girl's freedom. And as I thought more about it, a new discomfort took root within me. How many more lives were being ruined, and how many more girls were being sold while I tried to carry on with life as usual?

And so I entered a new phase in my life, one where I felt as if God was working behind the scenes, guiding me to discover more and more about the issue. It came up in conversation with friends, and I started searching on the Internet for information about this human tragedy. Gradually the mist began to clear. And when I heard about the work of a nonprofit, nongovernmental organization called the A21 Campaign, listening as they told story after story of girls caught up in this, my jaw was on the floor. This horror has a name—*human trafficking*—and it destroys too many lives. That was when I knew I had to do something.

I later learned that human trafficking was the "second largest global organized crime,"[1] generating about $150.2 billion each year,[2] more than the estimated profits of the tobacco industry, Google, big oil, and US banking.[3] As many as twenty-one million people—adults as well as young children—are used for forced labor while anywhere from three to nine million people are exploited in other ways, the bulk of them trafficked for the sex trade.[4] The average age of a girl sold to a pimp to be used repeatedly on the streets or locked away is twelve to fourteen years.[5] There have been reports of toddlers being sold for sex.[6]

The more I learned about human trafficking, the worse I felt. My old instincts of changing the conversation or going out and getting distracted didn't seem to work. Somehow, I wanted this. Somehow, I was ready for it. At age twenty-eight, I'd tasted my fair share of failed relationships and was beginning to work out that true satisfaction might not be found in a closet full of shoes and handbags. I wanted something more from life. I wanted to be disturbed. I wanted to be available.

For the first time in my life, I knew what it meant to be truly passionate about something. When I was a child, Mum built up a massive home library about diet, nutrition, and healthy eating. I wondered then whether I ever would be as passionate about anything as she was. But as I discovered more about the truth of human trafficking, I didn't care that people might think I was obsessed. I was on a mission, compelled by a sense of urgency. I had freedom where others didn't, and I needed to learn how to use it. Every day that passed without talking about it or trying to make a difference was another day that innocent people were enslaved.

Once I had spoken with everyone whom I knew that might know something about human trafficking, I started phoning organizations and asking if I could spend time with them, learning more about their work. I talked to people who worked with the victims of trafficking and saw the depth of the victims' suffering and the long journey to recovery for the ones who were rescued.

One man told me about Kamile, a girl from Lithuania. She was sold to a man who wanted her to work on the streets. He couldn't watch her all the time, so he needed to make sure that she wouldn't try to escape. He told her that if she tried to leave, he would find her and hurt her, and he would find and kill someone from her family. To prove that he was serious he pulled out some of Kamile's teeth with pliers and had one of her brother's fingers chopped off back home. She never tried to escape. Only through the work of an amazing organization was she eventually set free and— along with the rest of her family—allowed to rebuild her life in safety.

I found out about the role of the Internet. The technological wonder has created a new way for sex to be bought and sold. Criminals follow the trends, and they're now targeting young boys because of the big demand for sex.

Approximately thirty million people worldwide are slaves today.[7] Many of them are sex slaves, but many more work in brick kilns, in clothing factories, or on farms. The clothes we wear, the chocolate we eat, the phones we use, and the gold we cherish could bear the fingerprints of someone trapped in forced labor. Children are forced to beg with sedated babies that are not their own, and innocent-looking nail bars are often the business of choice for crooks who need to launder the money brought in by their girls. Women are raped, and their babies are sold to pedophiles. Then there is the rising trade in organ trafficking, where kidneys, lungs, and other body parts are sold by people who have no right to do so. Each new fact added to the appalling reports.

Soon after watching that movie I started to get serious about the details. I wanted to know more about why such a low percentage (1 or 2 percent) of victims is rescued and why so few European traffickers (one in 100,000) are prosecuted.[8] I wanted to know why a state-run children's home a few miles from where I grew up allowed children to be taken—believed to be sold into the sex trade and forced criminality and never heard from again. Why was this not major news?

So I started to do the rounds of the London organizations working in the sector, but I find out that it is hard to join in on the work to combat human trafficking. If you're passionate about homelessness, you can volunteer at a shelter, and if your heart burns with a desire to focus on those living with HIV/AIDS, there are probably clinics and organizations near you where you can offer assistance. But when you're passionate about helping those trapped in modern-day slavery, you can't just show up and expect to be given a badge and a serving apron. I understand why—the issues are so complex, and hands-on assistance requires extensive training—but it was frustrating for a newbie like me to hit so many closed doors.

So I continued my mission to talk to as many people on the planet as would talk to me about human trafficking. I moved my way up the food chain, starting with workers in nonprofit organizations, then meeting experts, lobbyists, and politicians. It became clear that it is our lawmakers who ultimately have the power to bring change, so when I got the chance to attend a press conference where a member of the British government was going to address the room about the forthcoming London Olympics, I jumped at it.

A couple of my brainy friends coached me on what to say. Nevertheless, I was still totally petrified as I raised my hand to ask a question. I got the nod, and I knew this was my biggest chance yet to get people talking.

"Minister," I mumbled, smiling nervously, "it's widely known that international sporting events like the Olympic Games attract so many visitors that it leads to a rise in prostitution. Therefore, the numbers of girls brought across borders against their will and forced into the sex trade will increase. What steps will the government take to ensure that London 2012 does not contribute to the rise in human trafficking?"

His answer was as smooth as the leather on his shoes. He didn't miss a beat as he talked about the problem being treated as a security issue. But it was not the public answer that I remember most; it was what he said to me afterward in private as the crowds leaked out of the room. "The thing is," he said, "not much is going to be done at all. There's so little that we can do to stop this."

I got the feeling that human trafficking is a little like Pandora's box. It's a problem that, once addressed, will take so many resources and occupy so much time to fix that the politicians would rather keep the lid on it as best they can. I can understand their reasons, but I can't accept that this is the very best I can expect from my government. I can't accept that we should give up and ignore the buying and selling of girls and boys.

Someone told me that governments aren't dealing with the problem as fully as they could because of the costs. It's an expensive business to rehabilitate a woman who has been rescued from the sex trade. Between housing, therapy, and gynecological fees, a former member of Parliament (MP) told me, the bill can easily reach six figures a year per person. Why spend the better part of $1 million helping five victims regain their humanity when you can lock up thirty burglars, rapists, or murderers for the same amount? The plain and simple truth is that there are no votes to be found in the fight against human trafficking. That means we need to lobby the politicians if we want them to make the necessary changes. We're going to have to make a lot of noise, win over a lot of friends, and work hard to put this horrendous failing into the political limelight.

One day I found myself face-to-face with a judge. "Why aren't more traffickers getting convicted?" I asked.

He paused before he answered. Lowering his voice he told me, "The laws to prosecute traffickers exist, but the police either don't know how to look for the victims or they just don't have the resources. You live in southwest London, don't you?"

"Yes," I said.

"How many British aristocrats and wealthy foreign nationals live near you?"

"I don't know. Must be hundreds," I said.

"But you don't see them every day, do you?"

"I suppose not."

"And what about brothels. Do you see any of those where you live?"

Brothels? I couldn't ever remember seeing one anywhere, let alone where I live. I shrugged and told him so.

"There are as many as three hundred brothels in action in one borough of southwest London. They might not be hiding behind massage parlors, but they're there all right. Hiding behind the neat doors of respectable apartments are girls and boys being raped for money."

His words stayed with me for days as I traveled home and tried to go about my life. But it was futile. I found myself in a state of mind that I'd never experienced before. I was going to work, hanging out with friends, and seeing what people were up to on Facebook, but living a normal life felt wrong. I was aware of an almost permanent frustration beneath the surface, like a mosquito bite at the point where your shoe meets your ankle. I was aware of the enormity of the challenge and the importance of changing the political view of the issue, and yet instead of feeling overwhelmed, some small part of me felt that I must expend all my energy on at least trying to make a difference on this issue.

Less than two hundred years ago our ancestors managed to abolish the transatlantic slave trade that saw millions shipped from Africa to the Americas, and today, the number of those tricked and traded far exceeds the number of those held in irons as they were sold to pick tobacco, cotton, and the rest. How have we let this happen? How can we turn a blind eye to it?

All these thoughts were only half-formed on the morning that Steph and I took our run, but as the idea of the row began to take shape, I had a growing sense that I needed to do it to do something good for the cause of anti-human trafficking.

So here I am, jumping up and down by the River Thames, talking and laughing manically about the fact that my best friend and I will one day climb into a little rowing boat and take ourselves across to the other side. I'm too excited to know it then, but soon enough I figure out that there's a reason I've spent the last couple of years reading, researching things that make me cry and talking to people about problems I'm far too small and ill-equipped to do anything about. There's a reason I feel as though my life has been hijacked by this cause, and there's a reason I'm caught up in the daydream of a transatlantic row. And that reason is called freedom. That's what I'm going to row for. That's why I'm here.

CHAPTER 5

The Stories We Tell

A dventure's in my DNA. When Mum was twenty-two she left the quiet Scottish community that had been her home and headed east to Pakistan, where she spent a year as a volunteer. In her free time she'd load up a cloth rucksack with a little food, a sleeping bag, and a good supply of head scarves and trek out from the city to discover the world beyond. She saw the mountains of Nepal, got lost among the crowds of Delhi, and traveled to places she'd never heard of as a child: Dhaka, Agra, Patna, and Banaras. Those were the last days of the 1960s, and the only other westerners around were hippies in search of good times, cheap drugs, and enlightenment. When Mum was ready to return to Scotland, she climbed aboard an aging bus that slouched lazily through Afghanistan, Iran, Turkey, and on to Europe. The trip took a whole week, but the adventure was worth every minute.

Dad also played a part in getting me into this row. He never traveled as much as Mum did, but when he was a teenager he was the best middle-distance runner in central Finland. He grew up in a rugged land knowing that when pushed hard, the human body is capable of going farther and faster than many would think. I'll need to draw deep on that determination in the coming months.

So when I tell my family about the row, I'm not worried about how they will react, but I still want their blessing. No matter what we've been through over the years, I know that if they're behind me on this row, it'll be easier.

That's why I choose to heavily edit the story about what an ocean row involves. Steph's ex-boyfriend completed the challenge a couple of years ago, and she told me horror stories about his crossing. He was obsessed with sports and often exercised to the point of throwing up, thinking that only then could he be satisfied that he had pushed his body to its utmost limits. With that level of drive and determination, he and a friend took on the waves and nearly lost. They ran out of food and rowed for a day only to be forced back five days by storms. Steph flew to Antigua so that she could be there when they made it to port. She ended up staring at the ocean for a whole month before they battled their way to their destination.

I'm a little nervous when I sit down with Mum to tell her about my plans. What if she freaks out? Could I really go ahead and do it without her support? Turns out I needn't have worried, as her reaction is perfect.

"Mum, Steph and I are going to row the Atlantic Ocean," I say.

"Really, darlin'?" I watch as her lips form a smile, which spreads into a laugh as the idea sinks in. "That's great!"

"You know I've never rowed before, don't you?"

"Yes, but you'll be fine, Julia. I know you can do it."

There's no lecture on the perils of the ocean and no long list of questions about the logistics of the voyage or the wisdom of our undertaking it. She doesn't question my lack of experience or my intentions. She's behind me all the way. When I grow up and have kids, I want to be just like her.

The day I tell Joy about the row, she's disbelieving at first. "You're going to row the Atlantic? Really? That's the kind of thing that I'd do, not you." She's right too. I'm known for my routines and the need to have everything ordered and organized, with my immaculate nails and matching shoes and handbags. She's the marathon runner, the outdoor type with the adventurous spirit. But she's behind me, and that means the world.

And Dad? Despite being confused at first, thinking that I mean to cross the Atlantic at the northern end, forcing my way through the worst of the northern hemisphere's wintry conditions (which he rightly tells me is both reckless and crazy), he's quickly supportive. Once we get the maps out and I show him the southerly route we plan to take, he gets it.

Steph is amazing at organizing things, and it doesn't take her long to persuade an ex-Olympic rower named Toby to teach us how to actually row. We never consider that we might not be able to do it, but in our favor, we recognize that we are at the wrong end of the learning curve. Secretly, though, we don't think that it is going to be too tough. How much of a challenge could it be?

A few weeks after that morning run when we decided to do the row, it's the start of October, and the summer is fading as Steph and I get ready to meet with Toby for our first training session. We're both full of optimism. My phone rings, and it's Dad. "Julia, you need to come home now. Mum's tried to kill herself."

Everything stops. For a second I am silent. Dad's words are in my mind like a sour taste that lurks in your mouth. Then I tell Steph that she'll have to go to the training without me: "I have to go home. Mum needs me."

During the forty-five minute drive, images tumble through my mind of what I might see when I arrive, even though Dad assures me that Mum is not in immediate danger. Yet when I slam into the driveway and spring through the door, I am not ready for this sight.

Wearing only her underwear, Mum sits on the stool in the kitchen. Dad motions with his hands toward her stomach and wrists, trying not to startle her as he shows me what she has done. There are cuts and open wounds but not much blood. He tells me that he found her trying to stab herself in the belly with a knife. When he took the knife away, she tried to bite her wrists.

Mum is quiet through this explanation. Her eyes are vacant, staring at something I can't see. She's never harmed herself before, but I'm not surprised that she has now. Since the start of the year her business has been struggling. Once, the front door of this house kept up a steady rhythm of clients asking Mum for advice on diet and nutrition, but over the last few months—since Mum made big changes—the work dried up. And as the business sank, it took Mum down too.

I swoop her up and hug her. "It's going to be okay, Mum. Everything is going to be fine."

Within less than a week we find out how wrong my words are. I'm at my apartment when I get another call that sets my heart racing. This time it's Joy's husband. They had been at my sister's home for my niece's birthday when Mum lost it. She broke down, started shouting, lashed out, and hit Joy repeatedly. Unsure of what else to do, they called an ambulance. The police turned up as well, and less than two hours later Mum was committed to the psychiatric wing of the nearest hospital. Joy spent the night with her, trying to help Mum sleep on a too-thin mattress in a too-bright room.

I visit her the next day and take over from Joy. My sister's face tells me the whole story in an instant: she looks traumatized and exhausted. Even though it's a newly built ward and the place is clean, I'm shocked at how cold and soulless it feels. It seems a place where recovery is a distant fantasy.

Mum's on the mattress on the floor, sitting up, but any resemblance to the mother I've known and loved my whole life stops there. She looks straight at me as I approach. "You're not the real Julia," she hisses. "You're pretending."

"I'm Julia, Mum. It's me."

"You're lying. Who are you really?"

The same question—about *her*—roars through my head. This woman in front of me might look like her, but when she talks she's a million miles away from my real mother. Where has Mum gone? Where is the woman who has always been so calm, so quietly wise, so able to hold it all together in spite of whatever is crashing around her? Inside I sob and scream, but outside I remain calm. I must not do something to frighten her.

The medical staff explains that her disorientation is a side effect of the antidepressants. They will take awhile to bring her back to something like normal. Meanwhile the best thing we can do is to be with Mum and remind her of how much we love her.

This now becomes the pattern of my life. Dad, Joy, and I make sure that someone is beside Mum throughout her waking hours. I start work at 4:00 a.m., getting to the TV studio and preparing the morning news program. Then I get back in my car and drive to this place that I hate and sit with my mother. I lose more of her each day.

She's on suicide watch, so the staff keeps an extra close eye on her. Despite the hopes of the staff and the family, her conversation gets darker, not better, with the passing of each day. A friend accompanies me one afternoon, and Mum tells us that the staff is cutting up the dead bodies in the hospital and feeding them to her. It's too much to hear, and I make my excuses as I search for a quiet room where I can cry.

As I start to notice other patients in the ward, I take a little comfort that most of them appear to be far more disturbed than Mum. She makes odd statements, but many others shout, hit themselves, or walk around like zombies. What really bothers me is their age. Most of them are about my age or younger. Why are so many people my age losing it? What's wrong?

By the time mid-October comes around the doctors approve the plan of moving Mum to another hospital, one closer to her home. If I thought the previous place was disturbing, I am stunned by this one. Pulling up to the building that sits like a giant cube of disused concrete, I immediately start to feel anxious about what we will find inside. After a ride in the rattling elevator I get my first glimpse of the patients. They are different from the last group. Many of the same behaviors are evident—the shouting, the hitting, the wandering—but there's an air of danger. Clothes are soiled, floors are filthy, and one woman—rake thin and haunted around the eyes—has hair matted with what looks like old food. The smell of disinfectant barely covers the odors of sweat and human waste. How did my mum, this woman of faith and wisdom, end up here among the young whose lives have been ruined by drugs, alcohol, or whatever else has taken them down? She is sixty-five. I thought that by then we were supposed to have it all together.

A couple of weeks into Mum's stay at the new hospital, it's clear that she's not responding to the antidepressants in the way the staff expected. She's lost all sense of taste, and she gobbles up the chocolate I bring her. Part of me feels bad for giving it to her, knowing that she has been a guru of healthy eating all of her life, yet seeing her devour a snack gives me a glimmer of hope.

One crisp fall afternoon I take her to Windsor to look at the castle, and I hope that the tourist-friendly location will give her mind something different to think about. I'm wrong. She spends the whole trip asking me why nature is dead and why mothers are pushing dead babies around with them in their strollers. It's as if she's reading a totally different story to me, one that's set against the same background and features the same characters but has a more sinister plot. She's living in a horror film. Instead of helping by bringing her out into this world, I've made her more scared. That scandalously filthy, broken-down hospital ward is the safest place she can be right now. I take her back, and my last ounce of hope drains from my heart.

In the midst of all of this, I've not been able to spend anything close to as much time as I should have on the row. My fitness levels are way too low and I'm still as much of a novice on the oars as I ever was. Can I make it across when I'm in a state like this? I doubt it, but somehow I believe that things will work out. After all, they have a habit of doing that. If the row's meant to be, it will happen.

CHAPTER 6

Are You Serious?

Having missed that first session with Toby, the ex-Olympic rower, Steph and I aren't able to find the time to meet with him until a few weeks later. It doesn't go well. I'm feeling overwhelmed by the sum of everything going on in my life, and Steph has just had a Brazilian hair treatment and doesn't want to put her hair in a scrunchie because she is worried it will kink. Toby is not impressed.

"Are you serious about this row?" he asks, staring at us with wide, unsmiling eyes. I feel like a teenager again and start to give in to the urge to sulk at the telling-off. We both mumble that we are, but I don't think any of us are all that convinced anymore.

Halfway through that session—with each of us on a rowing machine called an *ergo*—I finally know that what Toby means by the word *serious* and what I understand it to mean are two entirely different things.

He makes us row hard for 3,000 meters (10,000 feet)—about thirty lengths of an American football field. Then, just when we think we're done, he has further instructions for us. "You've just realized you're in a shipping lane and can see a tanker a few miles off. You've got to press on as hard as you can for another 3,000 meters. Got it? Right, go."

"He's not messing around, is he?" whispers Steph as we start. I smile back. Before long talking is beyond either of us.

She is right. Toby is a coach who turns good rowers into great rowers. We are nothing like his usual clients and need to be made into rowers in the first place. Forget about becoming a rowing great; can he even get us to the point of being good?

That session leaves me exhausted. My legs are on fire, and I'm dizzy as I try to walk. I've never been pushed so hard in an exercise class, and even though I'm completely wrecked, I've only been on the machine just over an hour. On the ocean I will have to do eleven more of those sessions every day for sixty to one hundred days—that's if the crossing is average. If conditions are worse, it will take longer.

My sense of dread grows as Toby explains that reaching basic levels of strength and stamina is good, but sitting on an ergo can never prepare us for the realities of ocean rowing where the wind and the waves will make it even harder and we will be wet, hungry, and scared.

Scared, huh? At least I know what that feels like. Fear and I know each other pretty well.

To make matters worse Steph is growing confused about the row, and I can understand why. We talk about it one day on a run.

"My family isn't very happy about it," she says.

"Really?"

"Yes. They just don't feel settled about it."

I try to think of something sympathetic and encouraging to say, but I get the feeling that this is one of those conversations where I need to listen more than speak.

"And every time I tell someone else about the row, I get the same reaction. They look all surprised and say things like, 'You're sure you want to do this?' or 'I'd never have pictured you trying such a thing.' It's starting to wear me down, Julia."

The two of us decide to get some help, so we visit some wise friends from church for a bit of advice and prayer. The trouble is, Steph walks away feeling flatter than ever. The day soon arrives when Steph and I have the talk.

"I can't do it, Julia. I can't do the row."

What do I say? Do I try talking her around? Somehow that just doesn't seem right. Do I tell her to sleep on it? I know she's been doing that for so long now.

As difficult as it is, I have to support her. "I understand, Steph. I love you, and I respect you. It must be such a hard decision to make."

Pause. That's not all I need to say. I take a deep breath and close my eyes before speaking again.

"But I'm going to carry on, Steph. I have to. I don't know how I'm going to do it or who I'm going to do it with, but if I don't row the ocean, something inside me will die."

Exhale. I open my eyes and look up at Steph. She smiles, we hug, and I know she's okay with the decision.

The moment is briefer than I expected. I should be used to it, though. It is just like the conversation Steph and I had as we stretched our legs beside the Thames. I'm gradually learning that not all life's biggest events are announced with fireworks.

On Steph's suggestion I call Simon, a guy we met a month or so ago. He founded the original Atlantic rowing race, which has become a biannual race across to the Caribbean, known as the Talisker Whisky Atlantic Challenge. I tell him about Steph pulling out and ask him my all-important question: "Do you know of anyone planning on rowing the Atlantic who might want to join me?"

"It's funny you should call," Simon replies. "There's a crew of six women who are attempting the women's world speed record, and they've just had someone drop out."

No way! "I'm your girl, Simon!" We talk details, and the news gets even better when I find out that instead of raising the $150,000 that Steph and I originally thought we would need for the two of us to get across, I need just $15,000 to join this crew. Could it get any better?

"They leave in January," he says.

It's midway through November, so that leaves me less than two months to get fit, learn how to row, and raise a suitcase full of cash.

"Are you ready for that?" he asks.

"Absolutely," I say.

I hate lying.

It seems impossible that in two months I could be on a rowing boat, preparing to undertake one of the most grueling physical challenges there is. Not only am I far behind in my preparations, I'm not sure if I can leave my family.

It's true that in the four and a half weeks that have passed since Mum was committed, she has made massive improvements and is finally well enough to be released from the facility. Life will have to be quiet and she will need plenty of care, but she can go home where Dad can look after her.

It has been a tough, tough season for all of us. Joy's daughter—my beautiful niece—is just two years old, and as hard as I've found it caring for Mum, keeping work together, training for the row, and thinking about sponsorship, Joy has had even more responsibilities. And Dad has had to watch his wife change before his eyes.

I finally have the chance to come up for air and do normal things: chat with my friends, take care of myself, refocus on my work. Do I really want to add "get ready to row the Atlantic Ocean" to that list?

I feel nervous every time I think about the row, but in a good way. These are the kind of nerves you feel when you fall in love, leaving you giddy at the thought of the wild adventure that awaits. No, I'm not ready yet, but I will be. I have to be.

CHAPTER 7

Which Way Is Up?

With the plan for Steph and I to row together now abandoned, and me now joining in with the all-female crew who is planning on setting a new Guinness World Record for the first all-female crew of six to row an ocean and breaking a record for the fastest-ever female crossing of the Atlantic, my training picks up. None of them live near me, so I'm training on my own; but with Toby overseeing my progress, I feel confident that I'm going to make it.

He doesn't see things quite the same way, though.

"Thanks for all you're doing to help me, Tobes," I say. "I'm going to be ready for this. I know it."

"I'll do everything I possibly can," he says. "Whether that'll be enough, I'm not sure."

We're outside a new venue for our training, and now more than ever I'm feeling the lack of preparation. I hardly did any training while Mum was in the hospital, only the occasional trip to the gym to work out on the ergo. The plan was to gradually increase the amount of time I could row at a sustained pace, starting with 30 minutes, through 45, 60, 75, 90, and up to 120. I'm still stuck at 45. I've lost weight due to the stress of the situation with Mum, and while ordinarily this would be a good thing, I'm actually supposed to start the row with extra muscle and fat reserves. Toby tells me that it's practically impossible to consume enough calories on the ocean, and the extra pounds will make all the difference. There's no fooling Toby, especially not once we get out on the water today.

We're at the Leander Club in Henley-on-Thames—the home of British rowing and backdrop to a lifestyle that is very far from mine. The club has been here since 1818, and today it's just as much a world of privilege and power, where everybody knows how to behave, as it has always been. They're all far too polite to actually say something when you make a mistake, but they all stare nevertheless.

"Uh, Toby," I say as he strides out of the boathouse toward the water. "How do I carry these?" He looks back and laughs at me. I'm struggling to work out which way to carry a set of oars and getting it spectacularly wrong. I smash another one into the doorway, narrowly avoiding decapitating some old guy in a blazer who looks decidedly curious.

Through the training sessions that follow, I meet many wonderful, supportive people while at the Leander Club, but others make me think that some of the guys who shark their way through the flat waters of the Ivy League look down on the ones who row across oceans. Maybe I'm paranoid, but it appears that flat-water rowers are all about grace, perfection, and discipline while ocean rowers rely on determination, guts, and the ability to keep going in spite of fear and failure. Until a few months before, I had honestly thought that my life was defined by my desire to make things look better on the surface than they were beneath it. These days, I'm all about learning from the fear and failure and keeping it real. I recognize that displaying my vulnerabilities demands far more courage than trying to convince everyone of my strengths.

"The thing is," says Toby one day, "you're nowhere near where you need to be right now."

"I know," I say. "But I'm getting there, Toby. I know it's going to be fine."

"No, it isn't, Julia. You're facing a challenge like nothing you've ever faced before. You're going to row for twelve hours a day, two hours on, two hours off, nonstop for two, maybe even three months. You're going to deal with waves as big as a house and seasickness that will leave you wishing you'd never started this thing. But you're going to have to keep on eating because your body's going to be the only thing that will get you out of there. So if you don't spend more time rowing now, you're just not going to be ready."

What do you say to a speech like that? I say nothing and pick up my oars again.

One weekend I take a survival training course with three of the UK-based girls who will row with me. We learn about ocean survival and practice pulling each other out of the water and into a mock life raft that's drifting around the swimming pool. The instructors share lots of information with us, but the basic news is this: It is dangerous out there. If your foot leash is not attached to the boat and you are swept overboard, it's game over. If there's a serious medical emergency—the sort that requires more than pain management—it's probably game over. If you need to be airlifted off the boat and you're in the middle of the ocean, guess what? It's game over.

None of this bothers me as much as it probably should. After all, I've heard enough horror stories to know the seriousness of the challenge. My optimistic spirit kicks in. Who cares if I'm being naive? I'm making a choice, and fear has no part of it. It's going to be okay. I know it will.

On November 23, I'm driving home from work when I check my voice mails and hear my sister. She's hysterical: "Get here *now*, Julia! I knew this would happen, and I've dreaded this day. He's attacked Mum."

I don't need to hear more to know who *he* is. I know I'll see him as I arrive at the hospital, and when I arrive Dad's looking pale, guilty, and awkward as he waits near the emergency room. I'm determined not to talk to him until I've seen Mum, so I walk straight past him. I find her in a cubicle beyond the nurses' station. She's lying on a bed, staring at the ceiling. She's shaking. Is it shock? Is it fear? A nurse stands over her, working carefully with a needle and surgical thread. Mum's hair is matted with blood. From the top to the rear of her skull, her skin is split open. It looks as if someone has run a knife across her head.

I turn to Joy, who is more distraught than I've ever seen her. Yet she smiles, her eyes full of tears. She's trying to pretend to Mum that it's all going to be okay.

"They think she hit her head against the doorjamb in the hallway at home," she says. "The paramedic told me there's a trail of blood that runs from the front door all the way along the hallway to the kitchen. Dad says Mum tripped."

Those last words, though whispered, hang in the air for ages. I look at my sister and know that she's thinking exactly the same thing as me: *How could she trip and fall that far and that fast against the wood?*

The nurse pauses, and I kneel down beside Mum. I take her hand, and kiss it. I try to remain calm as I talk to her. "Oh, my precious mummy. You're going to be all right. You're okay. You're okay."

As the nurse finishes stitching up Mum, we tell her that we think Mum was assaulted, and Mum doesn't correct us. She just keeps staring. After completing a bit of paperwork, we are free to take her away. I'm more relieved than I can say, but then it hits me. Where can we take her? Where can Mum go? She can't go back with Dad, but she can't be on her own. We decide to take her to Joy's house, and sobbing again, I follow them in my car.

I didn't think that life could get much worse, but in this moment it has. Panic about the row rises within me. With less than six weeks left before we start, will I still be able to make it? Will Mum bounce back and be right again quickly enough for me to pack my bags? And if she's not and I have to bail out on the row, what does that mean? I've spent the last six months of my life trusting that I was born to do this row. I've worked hard to get this far. What does it mean if I fail now?

By the time we reach Joy's house, it is late. We're all tired and in need of sleep. I join Mum in the guest room, sharing the double bed, but neither of us sleeps well. The painkillers they've given her don't seem to work, and she rocks and shakes as she cries out next to me: "My head, my head. It hurts. It's so sore."

All night her mood shifts like mist. At times the pain appears to be almost too much for her, but then she is lucid and able to talk. Then something inside shifts, and she returns to the frightened, confused woman who was with me at Windsor Castle a few weeks ago. She talks strangely for a while before she quiets down again. At one point her eyes widen, and she says, "I've never seen him so angry. I thought he was going to kill me."

The biggest shock is her face the next morning. At the hospital, she was pale, but she now has incredible bruising around both eyes. She looks like a victim of a horribly violent crime with balloons beneath her skin. The force with which she struck the doorjamb must have been horrendous. I can't imagine her pain. Her wrists show signs of bruising, and as Joy and I talk with Mum at breakfast, we piece together the story the best we can.

Mum had a habit of checking up on Dad when he worked in the garage, but it seems this time was different. Still medicated and confused, she continually peered around the garage door, hassling him. It might have had something to do with her phone; she mentioned to Joy and me that she had lost it—even though we knew it had been in her possession since she had come home from her commitment—and she could have panicked and accused Dad of taking it.

Dad probably got angry and ushered Mum back into the house. Increasingly unsteady on her feet these last few months, she could have tripped or been pushed over the doorway.

This is the closest we can come to working out what happened. But one thing is clear: whatever the cause of the injuries, Mum is not safe at home.

Mum goes to rest, and Joy and I discuss our mutual conclusion. Mum can't live with Dad, and she can't stay with either of us. In her fragile state she needs more help than we can give, and we acknowledge that we have to take her back to the psychiatric ward.

This has to be the saddest day of my life. The squat gray building, the aging elevator, the flakes of paint littering the floor—all of it speaks of a corner of life that everyone would rather overlook. And yet, for the second time in as many months, we leave Mum here, trusting her care to the people who run this place. They know that our decision is hard for us, and some of the staff are upset at seeing Mum again so soon, especially so broken and bruised.

I'm so desperately upset that I can't hide it from Mum. I've tried all along to be strong for her, to tell her that everything will be okay and that she's safe, but I don't believe those words anymore. I shudder as the tears flow. Is this what it feels like to give up a child for adoption? I'm not sure that anything else life has to throw at me can be harder than this.

I've gotten into the habit of praying silent, gut-wrenching prayers—I'm always too numb to pray out loud—each time I leave the hospital. But this time I can't even muster up the thoughts.

I drive home and park outside my house. Before I go in I must call Simon, the organizer of the transatlantic race and the man I phoned a few weeks earlier when Steph pulled out.

"Simon, I can't do the row," I say. "My mum's back in the hospital, and it's even worse this time. I'm sure she'll pull through, but I'm nowhere near ready to join the girls. I'm physically, mentally, and emotionally exhausted. I've got nothing left."

"It's okay, Julia. It's okay. I understand. Leave it to me and I'll tell them."

All I can say is, "Thank you."

CHAPTER 8

Unexpected

It takes two weeks for the bruising on Mum's face to disappear. By the time it does and after much deliberation, Joy begrudgingly goes to Australia for a month. It's only right that she join her husband who's working there and desperately missing his wife and daughter. Joy's been carrying so much, and I tell her a change of scenery will be good. She's a worrier, and being far away will be tough in its own way. Nevertheless, I'm glad she can get away. I've still not spoken to Dad.

The weather has turned far colder than usual for London in December. Snow is piling up, and the city is struggling to keep going. Yet every day, I get up at 4:00 a.m. and go to work, then drive out to visit Mum in the hospital. Sometimes, when the snow interferes with traffic, the forty-five-minute drive can take four hours.

The routine is always the same. We hug, and I ask her about her day. She tells me what little she can remember and asks me about mine. I struggle just like she does. I feel like a zombie.

I help her shower and do her nails. I read her magazines and talk about the weather. We don't talk about the row anymore. What is there to say about it?

After a few hours, we hug again, and I leave. As I reach the car, I look up. She always waves from the window.

I climb into the car and drive back. I eat, shower, and sleep the best I can before my alarm tells me that I must start the routine again. Most days I cry. How can a person produce so many tears?

Christmas Day 2010 approaches, and Mum has not been released from the hospital. Despite the shock I felt when I first visited the ward, I've grown to like and respect the staff, and I know they're doing a great job in difficult circumstances, but still there's no way that I'm going to let her spend the holiday in the hospital. The trouble is, I have to work. The solution comes when friends at church, who have been a constant source of kindness and support throughout Mum's illness, offer to pick her up, take her to the service, and sit with her as she attends the lunch that the congregation provides every year for anyone who is homeless, on her own, or in need of a warm, friendly place on the special day.

I join them as the meal finishes up, and they tell me how shocked they are to see Mum's state. She's there among the homeless and lonely of southwest London. Mum clearly finds the meal difficult. She is agitated and confused.

Back at my apartment, Mum seems a bit more like the person I remember. She stays with me a few days, and the improvement is evident. I guess being in a normal home where we can be mother and daughter again helps her. It doesn't matter that she's now the dependent child and I'm the responsible parent.

As with all parents, I'm aware of how hard it is to juggle different demands. As well as caring for Mum, I still have to give my best to my work, and there are still friends to see, church to attend, and some kind of life to live. But there's no room for the row. It has been wiped from my world. I was so convinced that it was meant to be, that God was fully behind it. The crew that Simon arranged for me to join has abandoned its speed attempt. For a moment I feel guilty about leaving them and worry that I ruined it for them, but I don't have the emotional baggage allowance to carry more sadness. I have to put it behind me.

Even though I dropped the idea of the row, not everyone has. Simon calls one day. "The girls have cancelled the row altogether. It wasn't just that you pulled out—there were so many things that didn't come together for them, and it was the right decision to make."

"Oh," I say.

"You know, you should think about putting together your own crew and doing the race yourself next year. You've got plenty of time, and you can still use the same boat that the original team was going to use. She's mine, and you can charter her from me."

It's a nice idea, and using this boat appeals to me. It's not just that I've done a bit of training in her already. More important, Simon's boat has made two successful transatlantic crossings. I never dreamed at the start of this idea that I would be able to have a whole boatload of people rowing to raise awareness about the horrors of human trafficking, and right now it seems unlikely. Very unlikely.

"It's nice of you to say that, Simon, but I couldn't get it together with Steph, and I couldn't get it together with the crew of girls. How many more signs do I need to tell me that I'm not going to row the ocean?"

Before the end of December something happens that makes me wonder whether the story is fully over. I travel to Egypt to attend a UN forum on human trafficking. I booked my flights long ago, and Mum seems stable enough in the hospital for me to leave for a few days.

At the forum, I grab my chance and stand up and speak. The room is full of experts, interested corporate types, and workers in nonprofits dedicated to the cause. Even Demi Moore and Ashton Kutcher are around. I'm not a natural public speaker, and my nerves cause my knees to shake.

I'm not sure what I'm going to say, but it comes out clear enough. I talk about the frustration of being passionate about the cause but struggling to find a way to make a tangible difference. Sports have always been my language, and it's the only source of the confidence I need to be doing any of this. As I bring my words to a close, I hear myself say something I've not rehearsed: ". . . and so that's why this time next year, I'm going to be rowing the Atlantic."

I'm shocked that I said it, but I distinctly heard myself say it. And so did a few thousand other people. Afterward, I have many great conversations, and—most amazing of all—I end up in conversation with someone from ManpowerGroup. By the time we're done talking they've offered to talk about sponsorship for the row.

I fly home, buzzing with excitement. I have no idea how it's going to happen or who will row with me, but I begin to find the faith that this row is going to happen after all. The dream begins to grow again.

CHAPTER 9

Preparation

The momentum keeps building as 2011 begins. Even though I have eleven months before the race, I barely have time to pull the row together. I pray continually for God's guidance and blessing. And the right help comes at the right time. A friend shoots a brief video of me talking about wanting to row the Atlantic, and my friends at work hold a quiz night to raise some of the extra money I'll need to get the row going. Between them they raise almost $10,000—enough for a deposit on the boat that Simon has offered to charter us.

That same video is put on the website for the race we'll be in: the Talisker Whisky Atlantic Challenge. The year is barely a few days old when I receive an e-mail from Sarah, an experienced rower who is keen to join me. I don't hesitate to say yes!

Mum has improved with me so much during the Christmas period. By the time Joy returns from Australia, we hope that Mum won't have to go back to the hospital. But because she's still a long way from being able to look after herself, Joy, her husband, and I decide on a new course of action. I'm going to move out of my apartment I share with Steph and move with Mum into a new place owned by my brother-in-law. She and I get on really well together, and she can be left on her own for a few hours each day.

Someone lends me an ergo, which I set up in the living room, and we start our new life together, with me spending hours rowing on the floor and Mum busying herself around me. It's classic mother-and-daughter time, and as I tell her about plans for the row, she seems to become part of it too.

By late February, winter starts to slip away, but still I'm exhausted and emotionally spent, so I decide to take a holiday to Dubai. It's a million miles away from rowing, hospitals, crowded freeways, and the general darkness and damp of London, and I love it. I'm at a party on a beach one night when I start chatting with this amazing woman named Katie. She's beautiful, funny, and highly intelligent. Katie moved to Dubai to set up something corporate and financial that I don't quite understand, but that's not what interests me about her. She explains that she's taken a year away from the corporate world in order to pursue a major sporting challenge. Since she hasn't decided on what that challenge should be, I smile and tell her about the row. I show her the video, and she's in!

I meet Debs when I visit ECPAT UK (End Child Prostitution, Pornography and Trafficking)—a nonprofit, nongovernmental organization. She tells me about their work and also taking on thirty sporting challenges when she turned thirty years old. When I explain about the row, she instantly says that she's in. The next day she e-mails to confirm that she meant what she said; she really wants to join the row.

I'm amazed. In many ways my life has never looked this chaotic: Mum and Dad aren't living together; I've given up my beautiful London apartment; I'm single and have no time for socializing; I live with my Mum who's painfully fragile; and I have calluses on my backside from the hours I spend on this ridiculous rowing machine. Yet this dream I've had less than a year, a chance to do something significant for a cause that I've been passionate about just a bit longer, is becoming a reality before my very eyes. I try not to let my excitement about the potential run away with me, but it feels absolutely wonderful.

Plans do not move forward without complication. Sometime around the time Katie signs up, someone else joins the team. She's a great person, and I love the idea of having her on board. As the weeks go by, however, it's apparent that her heart is not in it. She's graceful and brave when I ask her whether she can commit to this project, and she agrees that the best thing for all is for her to back out. If this row happens, there will be a whole load of people who never made it aboard but without whom it could not have happened.

I'm not a born leader or businesswoman, and I don't feel adequate to lead the crew that has formed. Consequently I make really basic errors. Even though Simon told me that I had to buy my way into the previous crew, I decide that when we enter this race, we should share the fund-raising to get to the start line. I don't mind if some people raise more than others—I want us to feel like a team, not passengers. I want everyone to feel as though they own it, as though they are all a significant part and not just a paying participant. It's a good aim, but I still end up worrying more about how to raise the $200,000 we need to charter the boat and pay for supplies, equipment, insurance, training, a PR firm, flights, and our race entry. I lose sleep over this. Lots of it. But passion pushes me through.

I have to become persistent in convincing people to join in and lend their support. It's a new skill, but the support seems to be coming in, and we easily find a replacement crew member. Kate is fresh out of university but as tough as an ox. She's exactly the sort of person we need. Helen, our sixth and final team member, is a natural athlete and—unlike the rest of us—an experienced flat-water rower. Even though we have only six or seven months left, she's happy to join up. Instead of my original plan of hiring a skipper, Sarah offers to step up. It's a big decision, but we've already bonded as a team, even though we've not been together in the flesh yet. Thanks to our weekly Skype meetings we have learned how to make decisions together. And since Sarah has plenty of experience being on the ocean, she's the obvious choice.

At last we have our full and final crew: Sarah (the one with the most experience of what it's actually like out on an ocean), Debs (tough as nails and stronger than any of us), Katie (mathematical genius and all-around wonder woman), Helen (an amazing athlete and great rower), Kate (the youngest member but with the most amazingly strong quads that could probably propel us across the ocean on their own), and me (who still doesn't really feel at all qualified to be on the boat).

As the preparations continue and the pace picks up, Mum is increasingly interested in the adventure. "What's happening today?" she asks most mornings. Usually I tell her about the brilliant crew and about meetings with experts and MPs who seem to want to help out in any way they can. Getting sponsors is a hard slog and test of perseverance, but whenever I open the morning mail and discover that a new sponsor has signed up, I shriek and do the running man in my dressing gown. Mum laughs and shares in the delight. One day I'm in the living room and I get a particularly surprising e-mail.

"What is it, Julia?" she asks, noticing that I've frozen to the spot. "What's happening, darlin'?"

I look up at her, my face full of smile. "We're going to meet the prime minister, Mum! We all get to go to Downing Street and talk to him about human trafficking!"

I've not seen her look so happy for the last year. We both do our little dance right there. I want the moment to last forever.

The row approaches, and I step up my training. Toby has helped me grow from a complete novice to a rower. But there are only so many freebies I can ask someone for, and I need to get as much time on the water as possible. So I thank Toby for everything he has done to get me this far and start rowing under the supervision of David, a sixty-something veteran rower. He's a genius, and I trust him from the start. I become his protégée, with his words ringing out across the still waters of the River Thames.

"Let your shoulders drop a little, Julia."

"You're burying that left oar too deep."

"Let your legs do the work, Julia. Push harder with your legs."

When I do what he says he shrieks with delight, filling the air with words of encouragement that I inhale for all I'm worth.

"That's brilliant! Most people take twenty strokes to put this kind of instruction into practice," he shouts. "But you do it straightaway!"

"That's because I don't have the time to wait for twenty strokes," I say. "I'm pretty desperate, David!"

The day David and I are on the water together and I finally *get it* remains one of the sweetest of my life. It's as if we start flying or as if someone flips a switch and all the gravity leaves the water. One minute we're heaving ourselves along or I'm catching a crab—a nice little euphemism for the times when I let the oar snag on the water as I'm hauling it back, slowing us down and spoiling the rhythm—but the next we're gliding through the water at what feels like incredible speed. David beams with an even bigger smile than usual.

In mid-October, six weeks before we leave for the little island of La Gomera—part of Spain's Canary Islands, where the race begins—we start to notice that the media are even more interested. There are numerous interviews to do for radio and magazines, and working with the media is another vital part of the row. My background makes me the obvious choice for many of these interviews, and I'm happy to do it. If we can give them a story worth telling, our message will travel much farther.

Members of my church have been supportive, and they offer to put on an event to raise awareness. I ask around to see whether someone will lend us a boat that we can park outside to get people talking, and a friend of a friend agrees to let us borrow his. My brother-in-law picks it up on a huge trailer and turns up with its owner, Joe, too.

Steph's been a great support throughout all this prep, and so she's there to help at the church. The moment Steph and Joe set eyes on each other, I know that something special is going on between them. And, yet again, I'm amazed at how not just the row but things around it seem to be blessed with a supernatural goodness. The event is a great success, with the whole church getting behind what we're doing. It's almost as if this row was meant to be, and nothing is going to stop it from happening.

Just a month before I'm due to leave for La Gomera the preparations become frantic. I struggle to find enough time to train, and I'm nervous when a good family friend phones me.

"Do you feel like an athlete who's in the very best shape she could possibly be?"

I decide not to lie. "I'm excited and happy and proud of all we've achieved so far, but I'm pretty exhausted. I feel as though I'm weak and overwhelmed. I've put in the physical training, but I'm mentally and emotionally shattered. I hope that I'll get a bit of a rest before the start."

"That's what I feared," he said. "You need to try to leave work right away and rest."

It's more an order than a suggestion.

I do what he says and almost immediately notice the difference. I move my flight to La Gomera forward by a few days and start trying to get my head around what it's going to be like to leave Mum behind. Over the months Dad has spent more time with us. He has been making the effort and trying to help Mum. It's not as if everything's perfect—when was it ever? He was just as scared as we were by what happened, and I know that he loves her too. I hope he'll remember that when things get tough. I'm still scared that something might happen between the two of them while I'm away, but I have to pray that everything ends up okay.

Saying good-bye to her is hard. "I love you, Mummy. I'm going to miss you so much," I say as I squeeze her little body into mine.

"I love you too, darlin'. I'm proud of you. You'll be fine."

I'm covered in tears and smiles, and I realize that it has been awhile since I felt as though I was the child and she was the parent.

The flight takes me south over England and down over the northern tip of Portugal. For most of the flight there's nothing but water beneath us. As I look out it begins to dawn on me that the vast spread of ocean that I can see is just a fraction of what I am going to have to row across in the coming weeks. I've never felt more nervous or more clueless in my life. I've prepared the best I can, and I've taken great comfort in the ocean-rowing wisdom that says, "The hardest part of the battle is getting to the start line." Judging by my struggles over the last few months, I hope these words are true.

I'm so naive.

PART 3

ROWING

CHAPTER 10

How Are You Going to Cope?

We've become like one of those couples caught in a marriage that is eating itself to death. Only we're not married, but we desperately need each other. What we're about to attempt is going to push each of us to the absolute limit. If we can't rely on each other, we're finished. And there aren't two of us in this relationship; there are six. At least there were six of us. As of today, we're officially a crew of five.

Sarah's had to drop out. It adds further volume—as if it were needed—to the question that has been echoing throughout each of our minds over the last few weeks: How are we going to cope?

People must think we're such a bunch of amateurs. For two weeks we've been on La Gomera. We've been wandering among the half-open restaurants and lonely palm trees, sharing the quayside with winter sun-seekers and the sixteen other crews who, like us, have decided to put themselves through hell and attempt the world's toughest rowing race (something that the event publicity continually reminds us). More people have climbed Everest than have done what we hope to do. More people have gone into space than have rowed an ocean. And a crew of six women has never done it. Or five.

For days we've not had our act together, not getting hands-on and becoming familiar with all the equipment, not been functioning as a team, and not been getting down to all the vital work that we've needed to do to ready both the boat and ourselves. We've been standing around at the marina, looking lost and wondering where to start.

It's only when Gemma—Simon's girlfriend—comes aboard to make her daily courtesy visit and check if all is well, that I swallow hard, take a swig of the sports drink I've been consuming so much that it's starting to turn my urine blue, and decide to tell her the truth. "We've got forty-eight hours until we're supposed to line up with sixteen other crews and begin our race to see who can row across the Atlantic the fastest. We're not in any way prepared and we've just lost our skipper. So, no, we're not okay."

Gemma holds her breath and bites her lip. "Meet me and Simon in the café in five minutes."

The five of us head for the palm trees and plastic tables. Not much is said as we walk. Losing a skipper means that we're going to have to rethink how we tackle the ocean, but we aren't really addressing that yet. We aren't anywhere near ready to squeeze ourselves into our twenty-nine-foot boat, get out there on the waves, and row ourselves about 3,000 miles, from this little island, at one end of the Atlantic, all the way over to Barbados (2,613 nautical miles). We're in trouble, and our oars aren't even wet.

I'd been leading the campaign, but once we arrived I handed over the leadership baton to Sarah, our skipper. I've probably not done as well as I might, but this is my baby, and letting go is hard. I hate the thought of standing by while things fall apart, so I prepare my speech for Gemma and Simon as we walk.

Over the last year I've gotten to know Simon well, and I feel as though I can be honest. Nevertheless, I feel nervous about what I have to say. The boat we're chartering from him is full of tiny holes and causing huge delays in our preparations, but that's only one of numerous things troubling me. We haven't trained on the equipment that's supposed to keep us alive: the GPS that tracks our progress, the Autohelm that steers according to the course we set, the watermaker that desalinates the seawater and makes it drinkable, the parachute anchor that we will unfurl into the water when we need to stop the boat from drifting when it's too windy to row, the satellite phone, and the battery tester. I'll tell them we have been so delayed that we haven't practiced beyond the marina where the waves start to pick up, and that is making me freak out.

I don't get a chance to say any of this, however. Simon has a speech of his own, and it's much shorter than mine. He says, "We wondered when you were going to speak up. The thing is, girls, if you crumble on land, how do you think you're going to cope out there in fifty-foot waves?" It's about all he says, but it's enough. Each of us knows that he's right. It's time for us to step up, pick a new skipper, and just get on with it. It's time to stop making excuses.

We head back to the boat, just a little more confident. Maybe now we stand a chance of making it across the ocean fast enough to break the Guinness World Record—which is a plan that has been evolving rapidly over recent weeks. The current record for the fastest all-female crew crossing the Atlantic stands at fifty days, and we really have to be at our absolute best to beat it. Maybe this is the final barrier we need to break through to let that happen. Maybe now we can do what we came here to do.

We get back by the boat and start to tackle the jobs that have piled up, though not everyone responds the same way. Katie seems ready to get on with things. Kate is quiet (but I'm learning that's nothing to worry about). Debs looks troubled while Helen's a bit teary. So am I.

This last year with Mum has been such a crazy ride, but I'm finally here, standing on the marina looking at our boat. We call her *The Guardian*, and I'm praying that she's going to look after us in the coming weeks. The first thing we have to do is unload Sarah's stuff. None of us have loaded our personal kits on yet, so there aren't really any clothes or toiletries of hers to remove, but there's a whole lot of food to find and take off. All of us have selected, double-bagged, and stored our daily food packs carefully around the boat. They're expedition foods, specially designed to provide maximum calories with the minimum of preparation required. We'll just have to rip open the bags and add boiling water. As for what the Thai curry and spaghetti bolognese will actually taste like once we're weaving about on the ocean, I have no idea. But it seems kind of fun.

Helen and I are the only ones who have no special dietary requirements, and we've spent four days getting the packs ready. Taking one-sixth of them off the boat seems like a waste of time, but we have to do it. We need the boat to be as light as possible for the speed record attempt.

We have to take off Sarah's life jacket with her name painted on the back, as well as her personal medical kit. We decide to peel her name from her personalized oar. It's going to be hard enough to make the crossing without her name staring at us with every stroke. It only takes one of us to do this, so Kate and Katie deal with the holes that are all over *The Guardian* like spots on a Dalmatian. Each hole needs to be cleaned and filled with marine glue. The process is only slightly more complicated than an activity you'd find in kindergarten, but filling these holes is vital. Debs and

Helen work on the equipment, taking out the watermaker and GPS to get to know them.

We're happy. We finally work together as a team and get things done.

And yet it doesn't take much for us to feel as though we're frauds. Someone—I'm not really sure who, only that he definitely isn't a rower—approaches me on the marina later in in the evening. "You're with the girls, aren't you?" he says. I tell him I am and watch as his face adopts one of those looks that's half frown, half smirk. Maybe he's heard about us losing our skipper, or perhaps he's seen us messing about with the disco classics blaring out of the stereo as we've been repacking. Whatever's behind it I don't know, but he says, "You're not really a proper crew though. You're just having a laugh, aren't you?" before wandering off.

I feel a bit deflated but not for long. Yeah, he's right. We're not a proper crew. We're not rowing purists. We all have an agenda, and we're determined not to waste this opportunity. But if we do it right, if we make it to the other side faster than any all-female crew has ever rowed it, a tiny shaft of the media spotlight will fall on us. And that could make a difference.

I care more about the media than I do about learning how to tie bowline knots. Because I know that whatever media attention we get won't last long, I will use every single chance to tell people why I'm here. I'll tell them about the dirty little secret that plagues our societies, ruining innocent lives and trying to destroy hope. I'll tell people that slavery doesn't just exist—it thrives today. I'll tell them that there are more slaves on earth now than at any other time in history. And I'll tell them that we abolished slavery once before, so why can't we do it again?

I'll tell them: that's why I rowed the ocean.

CHAPTER 11

Forty-eight Hours to Learn It All

D ressed in our pristine white polo shirts that are splashed with the names of the corporate sponsors who have paid for much of this whole adventure, we leave the hotel. As the morning sun showers down its sparkles onto the boats and still waters, we head down to the marina and toward *The Guardian*, our aging fiber-glass rowing boat that we trust to carry us across the Atlantic. She looks good with the logos of some of our sponsors plastered across her: our headline sponsor, ManpowerGroup, as well as all our gold sponsors—Red Button Design, LexisNexis, Logicalis, Warson Fine Beef, and Dubai Duty Free. It all feels more real, somehow. Crowds are everywhere, people smiling and hugging and taking photos as they cluster around other crews who, like us, are wearing their own pristine shirts.

It is December 5, 2010, and thanks to a last-minute change in the weather to the south, it has been decided we are to say good-bye today. It's the official start date of the 2011 Talisker Whisky Atlantic Challenge—a challenge that is as simple as it is tough: crews of any number row themselves across the Atlantic unassisted and unaided. That means no sails or anything that could act like a sail. Just the crew and their oars. There's a support boat making the crossing at the same time, but if you receive any help at all from the race organizers on board *Aurora*, it's game over.

There are a few people I really want to hug; they are in other crews that I've connected with while we've been waiting on La Gomera as well as in the months leading up to the big show.

I find Ross and Hugo first. I've grown really close to these twin brothers lately. Hugo hit his head in a swimming accident six years ago, broke his neck, and spent months recovering in the hospital. Along with two other friends, rowing the Atlantic is their way of raising money to fund medical research. They're young—barely out of university—but I know them well enough to understand that they're driven by something greater than a desire to win. They're determined to push themselves as hard and as far as they possibly can in order to make a difference in the lives of others. They are idealistic and crazy and probably a bit naive, and I feel the same way.

A big crowd has gathered around my other favorite crew: Row to Recovery. They're ex-soldiers. Two of them are fully able, three have lost a leg, and one is a double amputee. Six men, eight legs, one boat, and 3,000 miles—that's what they keep reminding people, always bringing the story back to the heart of the matter. They aim to raise $1,500,000 to help others who have been wounded in the line of duty. They do not call for pity, and they do not need sympathy. They just want to row, raise some money, and show that they can achieve the extraordinary beyond injury. Four of them are lucky to be alive, and they've chosen to break all the rules about what people say is possible. If they're crazy, I don't want to be sane.

We climb into our boats, feed our eleven-foot oars into their locks, and make our way out of the marina, toward the harbor wall that holds back the worst of the Atlantic. One by one the crews line up at the imaginary start line, wait for the single blast of the Klaxon horn from the race organizers, then slowly pull toward the ocean.

I feel a little sick, not from nerves or seasickness but from frustration mixed with elation mixed with sorrow. Although this is the start of the row for the other crews, it is not the start for us. We may be saying good-bye, but we're not going anywhere. Not yet. Race rules allow speed-attempt crews to start at any point within a two-day window in order to get optimum weather conditions, so we've decided to delay our departure by forty-eight hours. We want to take a shorter, more direct route to Barbados—not like the rest of the crews leaving today, heading for huge seas, and dropping south in the hope of picking up the southerly trade winds that will push them across. The truth is that we desperately need these days to do any number of jobs, including patching up the holes in the boat, repacking the supplies, and working out how to operate the equipment that will save our lives.

The last of the crews get their Klaxon start and leave us behind. Slowly, silently, the five of us row back to the marina where we tether up *The Guardian* and slip as inconspicuously as possible onto dry land. Suddenly I'm embarrassed to be in my pristine white polo shirt.

One good thing about being the only crew left in the marina is that we have the undivided attention of Simon, the support team, and the race organizers. Together we stand around *The Guardian*, looking her up and down as if she was a used car waiting at auction. Given the fact that she's covered in more than twenty tiny holes—not quite big enough to squeeze your pinky into—the used car comparison works. She's the one that nobody wanted, the one that got left behind. I know how she feels.

But we didn't get this far by feeling sorry for ourselves or by being overwhelmed by the challenges ahead. We got here by sweating, crying, and squeezing a mountain of tasks into a tiny window of spare time. It took a year and a half of twists and turns, of last-minute changes and unforeseen problems, but we got here. There's no way we're going to fall apart now.

The first decision is whether to have a skipper. Sarah was the obvious choice because of her ocean-sailing experience, but not one of the rest of us has been in charge of an ocean row. Furthermore, not one of us has rowed more than a few hours out there. We're all beginners in a way, but we agree that we need a leader. Eventually tough calls will have to be made, and the prospect of trying to reach an agreement while the waves threaten to take us down doesn't seem wise.

Because Debs was originally going to be the first mate, we decide that she should be skipper, with Helen stepping up to be first mate. The two of them have been amazing with the technical and practical aspects of the boat while we've been in La Gomera. Yet inside I can't deny that the decision concerns me. Part of the struggle to get to this point has been navigating the sharing of power. Give five or six fit, competitive women a challenge that many people say they cannot do, and they will dig deep to prove the naysayers wrong, which is what we've done all along. Sometimes the rock-solid determination and iron-plated competitiveness have made things awkward between us. Often, I'm the spokesperson for the team, which causes tension as well as self-doubt within me. I choose to trust that we'll make it across okay.

Our route is made up of twenty-one waypoints that need to be programmed into our GPS. As long as we stay within a one-hundred-mile corridor north or south of each point, we should be fine. Working this all out is called *passage planning*, and while Debs, Helen, and Katie get down to it, I turn my attention to the boat. Kate's dealing with the holes, and I'm almost finished with the supplies. Then I look at what I'm taking, and it doesn't seem enough: two hats, two pairs of shorts, one long-sleeved top, one short-sleeved top, a pair of salopettes, one sailing jacket, a few unopened letters from home, a personal medical kit, and that's about it. I'm not used to traveling so light.

I'm the one you see at the airport, suitcase open on the floor at the check-in kiosk, hands trying to transfer those extra pounds from my suitcase into my carry-on baggage. I'm the one who over-packs for a day out. I can't see the point in taking two pairs of shoes when my bag has room for four. And I have big hair, so if I don't treat my head right, I'll arrive in Barbados with my hair dreadlocked.

Since Debs has pale skin she has been allowed extra sun lotion, and Kate's intolerance for dairy means that she has a bulky alternative to our NASA-developed protein shakes. I put it to the others that my big hair qualifies as a similarly significant medical issue, and I have been allowed to take a bottle of hair conditioner. But I'm still not happy, so I sneak in a couple of extra dependables: hydrating facial gel and my iPhone. We agreed not to take personal phones because important numbers are programmed into the satellite phone. My phone is my life when I'm on land. Even though I know it's naughty, my small act of defiance helps me feel a bit better.

Our remaining thirty-six hours on dry land are unremarkable. We check the boat more times than we need to, we talk a lot about what it must be like for the other crews who are on the ocean, and I fret about someone discovering my contraband.

The night before we leave, we meet Gemma and Simon in the

Blue Marlin. The local café with its free Wi-Fi has the names of all the crews that have taken part in the row over the years scribbled in Sharpies on its walls. We're invited to add our names, but before we do, Simon has something to show us. Spinning his laptop around to face us, he points to the website that tracks each crew. We've been checking it on and off since yesterday, and we know which color line represents which crew. Our pink blob is still just a single dot held fast in La Gomera, but the others are all over the map. A few hours ago they were a fairly orderly collection of straight lines heading southwest. But now they're a crazed jumble of loops and twists. Whatever weather they've encountered, it must be big.

I'm shocked. I know the sea can be powerful, but seeing these lines brings it home in a whole new way. The boats look as if a giant has stirred the waters and created chaos into which the crews have been drawn. I look at Debs, Helen, Kate, and Katie, each wearing the same wide-eyed, slack-jawed expression as mine. Simon, on the other hand, has a smile as big as a sunset.

"They've hit some rough seas out there," he says. "I bet they're absolutely loving it."

CHAPTER 12

The Acceleration Zone

Our row begins without much fuss. In the forty-eight hours since the departure of the other crews, most of the friends who came out to see them and us have left the island on their pre-booked flights. Katie's mum and aunt remain, however, to cheer us on from another boat while we do our final checks. Kate and I make continual trips to the bathroom in the ferry terminal. I manage to do a last-minute phone interview with one of our Sky Sports News presenters. It feels strange to be talking with someone I know so well in London, just minutes before I climb into the boat and give myself over to the ocean. My knees literally knock, and I feel nauseous. I doubt that is one of my better interviews.

It is time to go. I hand over my flip-flops to Gemma, call Joy and Mum and tell them I love them a million times, and climb on board, shoeless for the duration of this next adventure. A moment of stillness settles on us in the early morning as we count down the seconds before the Klaxon horn issues its cry, and we slowly make our way toward the ocean that lies beyond the harbor wall. For the first time of many, I pray the words of Isaiah 43:2, claiming its promise: "When you pass through the waters, I will be with you" (NKJV).

Standing precariously behind Katie as she rows, I call out, "We're doing it, girls! We're really doing it! We're rowing the Atlantic!" I'm a little premature, because as we pass the man-made wall that shields the harbor from the worst of the ocean, the boat suddenly jolts and I stumble. It's as if we've been plugged into a different sort of power that sends the boat pitching from side to side.

People have told us about this point where the ocean pulls you toward itself. At first you're rowing out of a marina, fully in charge of your speed and direction, duped by the idea that you're in control. And then the ocean reminds you of the essential fact that you're not. No combination of boat and oar and human muscle will be able to win against the force of the ocean. You might catch a break and you might make it all the way across, but never believe that you have tamed the waters.

Like the ache that comes when you are separated from someone you have fallen deeply in love with, like the shock that follows your first car crash, the moment when the ocean currents drag you away from land offers a valuable lesson. It reminds you that you're committed, it tests your resolve, and it makes it perfectly clear that there is no turning back.

They call it the acceleration zone, and every ocean rower knows about it. While it makes the first minutes of our row a little easier, we know that we will have to do battle against similar forces and currents at the very end of our journey. But we have a long, long way to go before we reach that point. Right now, less than an hour into our epic voyage, I'm thinking about the acceleration zone and hoping that this row isn't a colossal, crazy mistake.

I retreat to the smaller of the boat's two cabins. It's situated at the front of the boat, and it's tiny. Imagine a sleeping bag made especially for a power lifter—not too long, but wider around the chest and shoulders than most regular people would need. Now imagine that sleeping bag inflated. That's pretty much the size of this cabin. Beneath me is a thin camping mattress, and to each side are two small bags. One contains everything that I have brought with me; the other one belongs to Katie. She and I have this fore cabin while Kate, Helen, and Debs take turns sharing the aft cabin. Theirs is bigger, but I suspect that I'm going to appreciate having this little space to myself while Katie's rowing.

For the next couple of months, she and I will share this space. For two hours Katie will take up her oars and row along with Helen while I lie here in the cabin. Then we will swap over, and Kate and I will take over. Debs will spend one day rowing with Katie and Helen and the next, rowing with Kate and me. Twenty-four hours a day, for as many days as it takes, we will do this, swapping every two hours to retreat, wet and exhausted, into this tiny space.

This space—which seemed so adventurous, so cozy when I first saw it—now feels far too small and uncomfortable. Other crews have thick, comfy mattresses, pillows, and other items to make their crossings as comfortable as possible. Comfort is an unnecessary luxury for us. We want the boat to be as lightweight as possible, so every extra pound makes a difference.

Pictures are allowed. But even though I've pinned up photos of the people I love, as well as messages, Bible verses, and quotations from which I have drawn strength over the years, this place feels alien to me. At home I have 150 pairs of shoes. Here I have none. At home I have windows, but not here. The only way in and out is through a hatch the size of a small suitcase, which we're supposed to keep shut at all times in case a wave breaks over us. If that happens it could flood the cabin, ruining what little stuff we have and putting us in a whole lot of trouble.

The idea of rowing the Atlantic might sound glamorous and exciting. The truth is that for exactly half my time I will be stuck in here, unable to stand or kneel. What am I going to do with myself? I'll read the one book that I've brought with me—my Bible—and I'll listen to whatever I've loaded onto my iPod. I'll sleep, I'll eat, and I'll write in my journal, but what else? I guess I'll spend a lot of time looking back at these smiling faces that have been stuck to the walls. Half of them I know and love, like my family and friends, but the half belonging to Katie I do not know.

Before we got to La Gomera, we'd only met as a team a handful of times, but through all those weekly Skype calls from our locations across the globe and the hundreds—probably thousands—of e-mails, I feel as though I know these girls well. Besides, I'm on a boat that measures twenty-nine by seven feet, with no prospect of a bath or shower for I don't know how long. Our greatest physical luxury is a blue plastic bucket to be used solely as our toilet. Odd is my new normal.

———————

Debs calls time as the first watch draws to a close, and I clamber out of the cabin and go through the changeover drill that we have practiced in the marina. I make my way to the bow seat nearest our cabin and attach my foot leash. When we were doing this on the still waters within the harbor wall, the boat felt stable enough for me not to worry too much about where I placed my feet. That has changed now. I'm glad for the foot leash because the boat feels far less stable than it should be. The waves seem to want to shake us, to remind us that we have absolutely no jurisdiction out here.

This is what is supposed to happen. Katie moves off the seat, and I take her place, my back to the tiny cabin we share. I place my feet into the foot plates and strap in each foot with the Velcro straps, which we have customized with sheepskin. Doing this every two hours is a hassle but worth the extra comfort provided by the sheepskin. We have also added foam to heel cups to protect from blisters. Once I'm sure I'm in the right position and as comfortable as I can get, I check that Kate is okay and push out my oars. The reality of this first changeover is frightening and hilarious in equal measure. For Katie to get out of her seat and for me to get into it require us to move in time, keeping the boat perfectly balanced as we place our bare feet in gaps that are just large enough. And with the waves playing with the boat and the spray showering us in salt water, the whole maneuver is crazily difficult. It's like playing Twister on a too-small trampoline. But we manage it. Surely we'll get better at it, won't we?

The hours pass, and we inch away from land. I don't know what I expected from this first watch—perhaps nerves mixed with a bit of excitement. I've got both of those in addition to feeling very, very small. Small in this boat against the size of the ocean, my oars making small progress with each stroke, my courage way too small for the task ahead. I also feel small in relation to history. This row may well be the most significant challenge I ever tackle, and we may break a record or two, but rowing the Atlantic is nothing new. Millions of others have made this journey west from the coast of Africa to the Caribbean. My foot leash is plastic and can be removed at will, but they were held fast by chains and locks and flesh-biting metal.

The transatlantic slave trade is over, but something harder to spot has replaced it. People still cram their slaves onto boats; only these days it's done in secret. One thing hasn't changed, though; today's slaves are every bit as powerless as the ones who sailed these waters long ago.

———

Two hours pass fast when you're rowing but slow when you're staring at the walls twelve inches above your head. As the first day fades away, I find the beginnings of a rhythm. I think I'm happier on the oars than off them. I close the hatch door behind me in the cabin, and a new feeling grabs me. It's fear.

It starts with the noise of the water. Two hours ago when I was in the cabin, the sound of the water barely registered. But now, as the darkness suffocates the boat and we can see only what our low-energy lights can reveal, I'm aware of how loud the ocean is. It's not the wind; it's the slap and drag of the waves as they hit the side of the boat. Like a clap from thinly gloved hands, followed by a hissing sound, the waves prod and push us constantly. There's no way to block out the perpetual reminder that we are guests upon these waters. Like a crowd of rioters crushing around a slowly moving car, the waves press in on us from all sides.

This fear is not a sudden, sharp emotion making my adrenaline kick in. My body knows that there is no way of getting out of this thing quickly. All we can do together is fight our way across. We can't take on the whole ocean, but we can pull ourselves through, one stroke at a time. This fight will be slow—a war of attrition. Slowly the ocean will try to win, pushing us this way and that, gnawing at our strength, pressing against our weak points, exposing our failings.

It's such a long way, and this cabin is so dark and so small. I'm not at all sure that I've got it in me to make it. I feel emptied of all the confidence and self-belief I'd fed on during the previous months.

CHAPTER 13

Stories in the Waters

The advertisement was published in 1896. Legend has it that it was an outrageous offer—the chance to win $10,000 (about $500,000 in today's dollars)—but some today believe that the reward was simply a pair of medals and a shot at glory. Whatever the truth, those were desperate times, and the twenty-year economic depression was fresh in most people's minds. The man making the offer (a newspaper owner named Richard Fox) wanted something breathtaking in return. He wanted someone (or more than one) to row all the way from New York in the United States to Le Havre in France.[1]

History doesn't tell us who else stepped up, but we know that two Norwegians—Frank Samuelsen and George Harbo—were crazy enough to blow their life savings on a rowing boat named *Fox*, with oak timbers for ribs and white cedar planking, three pairs of oars, some oilskins, and a frying pan. They left New York on June 6, 1896, and after fighting mighty gales, capsizing, losing vital equipment—including the frying pan—and going without sleep for days at a time, they made it to the Isles of Scilly, southwest of Cornwall, England, in fifty-five days.[2]

It was an amazing achievement, but the story doesn't have a happy ending. Even though Fox went to Paris and held a dinner in honor of the two rowers, handing each a gold medal in celebration, he never parted with the $10,000 prize money. Still, for 114 years nobody was able to cross the North Atlantic faster than Samuelsen and Harbo.

Maybe it's the Viking DNA that draws the Scandinavians to ocean rowing, or perhaps it's the love of nature, space, and extreme weather. Either way, the two Norwegians started something.

One of the greatest of all ocean rowers was Anders Svedlund. In the early 1970s the Swede crossed the Indian Ocean in sixty-four days,[3] then moved on to an even greater challenge: the Pacific. His story is more compelling because he was a purist, relying on less technology than Samuelsen and Harbo had. They had a compass and a quadrant and kept a daily log, but Svedlund took no radio and no other navigational tools. He climbed into his little plastic boat, pushed off from the coast of Chile, and headed west, following the sun.[4]

Svedlund rowed fast, and he rowed unlike anyone else. He was a vegetarian so he took no fishing equipment, just the basic food he could stock up at whatever island he stumbled across. He slept a full ten hours a night, trusting that his boat would turn herself toward the wind and avoid capsizing. His only regret about the boat, he told friends, was that she pitched and rolled so much it was impossible for him to stand on his head for any length of time. According to him, standing on your head for at least an hour a day was one of life's essential ingredients.[5]

He died in 1979. Living on land was disagreeable to him and dragging him down. Before he could get back out on the waters, he had a terrible fall in his kitchen, striking his head on a table and dying on the floor.[6]

The manner of Svedlund's death didn't match his life, but there are others whose epic voyages have ended in disaster. Not many have died on the ocean, but there have been six cases of ocean rowers lost at sea. Most of the time the bodies are not recovered, though somehow the boats always make it back to land, drifting in like riderless horses long after the end of a race.[7]

The saddest story I know belongs to Nenad Belic, a sixty-two-year-old cardiologist from Chicago. Like Svedlund, Belic wasn't attracted by the idea of publicity or influence. It was a challenge calling to him personally, even though he wasn't able to explain why he was doing it. He told a reporter before he left Cape Cod that the whole thing was a mystery. But he had been talking about rowing across the Atlantic for years, and sometimes a man just has to get out there and do it. Isn't there always something mysterious about chasing dreams?[8]

Belic invested heavily in a unique boat. It was fully enclosed, designed to protect him from the elements and to be self-righting in the likely event of capsize. He painted it canary yellow and named it *Lun*, as in *lun*atic.

Starting on May 11, 2001, his first three weeks were a tough struggle against the elements, and he made only sixty miles before the month's end. Had he started farther south he might have been picked up and swept along by the Gulf Stream, but Belic wanted to begin at Cape Cod, so that's where he began. The stubbornness is common to all ocean rowers, and that single-minded determination has the power to be both a great asset and a fatal flaw.

By the time he approached the coast of Ireland four months

later, Belic was surviving on food donated by passing vessels. As summer gives way to fall, and the hurricane season kicks off, the Atlantic becomes a far more dangerous place. Storms can become violent. Belic was only a few days away from land, but he was also headed for a monstrous storm. Ignoring advice to call the Coast Guard for help, he carried on. He was in the middle of a storm with wind gusts raging at almost sixty miles per hour and waves higher than twenty feet. He chose to wait, leaving a message with the Ocean Rowing Society to say that things were tough, but he had dropped his sea anchor and was waiting it out.

Nobody knows what happened next, apart from the fact that three days later, on the last day in September, the local Coast Guard picked up *Lun*'s distress signal. A Royal Air Force aircraft flew out and found the emergency beacon floating in the water, but no sign of the boat and no sign of Belic. The search intensified, with other crews scanning the water, but they found nothing. The weeks passed, and as the official search was scaled down, Belic's family did what they could to encourage local fishermen, pilots, and sailors to keep an eye out for any sign of the boat and the man who had pulled it so far across the ocean.

In mid-November, two commercial fishermen found *Lun*. She was floating upside down, drifting a quarter mile off the Irish coast. Divers were sent to check for a body, but though they found Belic's passport and wallet, they found no body.

How he died is a mystery. Perhaps he was swept into the ocean as he activated his distress signal; perhaps a wave burst through an open hatch. Nobody knows, and with no logbook recording his progress, *Lun* had none of Belic's secrets to share.

I look at the four girls on board this boat with me, and I see some of the same characteristics that united Belic and Svedlund.

We're all determined, and we're all obviously a little bit crazy. We are not qualified to do this, but everyone on this boat believes that we can do it. Nobody had to be persuaded to get on board. We all jumped at the chance within minutes of first hearing about the idea. We're confident that our fitness will get us much of the way and that when exhaustion, injury, or illness slows us down, our stubborn determination will get us the rest of the way.

But there are major differences between us and these legends. We're not alone out here, and the competitive spirit is strong within us. We'll fight to do our best, not wanting to lose face in front of each other. We don't want to be on the ocean for as long as it takes; we want to get off it as quickly as we can. For Helen, getting in the record books for being the fastest all-female crew to cross the Atlantic (and the first crew of five to cross any ocean) will satisfy the passion and drive burning within her. That makes her the best sportswoman among us. She's the one who couldn't sleep at night if she missed the final sit-up during a workout.

Kate's the one we call the Pocket Rocket. She's in her early twenties and small, but her thighs can pump out power like you wouldn't imagine. When we were on land, she did squats for fun, and since rowing is about 65 percent legs and not nearly as much in the arms as people think, she's going to help a lot. Debs is similar, with a physique that's tough and designed for no-nonsense hard work. She's not going to let discomfort get in the way.

Katie has two degrees in math and a background in city finance. I was always a middle-grade student who could have done a whole lot better, and I stumbled into a media job. But both of us have big hair, both of us like to look nice, and both of us have way too much pink in our wardrobes. And both of us are convinced that we can do this.

Above it all, this one difference separates us as a crew from the tragic stories of the solo rowers who have lost their lives: we're driven by a cause. For this effort to be worthwhile, we have to reach the other side in order to start telling people about why we did it. We have to make it, no matter what the struggles, no matter how big the waves or how fierce the storms.

CHAPTER 14

Things Fall Apart

This red bucket that I'm staring into fills my field of vision. All I can see is red. All I can smell is the blend of new plastic and salt water. All I can feel is the urge to throw up. The boat lurches up and down another wave, and I close my eyes. I've lost the battle once more. Let's just get this over with.

It started as soon as we were on the ocean proper, although I tried to ignore it, telling myself that it wasn't happening. But I knew I was in denial. I felt sick.

Until I started rowing, the smallest boat I'd been on was probably a five-hundred-foot-long ferry that shuttles tourists and big trucks between England and France. That makes me the least likely transatlantic rower ever, and the prospect of spending so much time getting flicked around by the waves has worried me for months. People seemed to line up to tell me how bad the seasickness would get. "You'll want to shoot yourself or jump overboard," said someone who'd been out here. "But don't worry, it will pass. And once it's gone, it's gone."

While I tried to take comfort from the advice, it never helped. I prepared by bringing a whole load of pills and a set of special wristbands that promised to limit the nausea, but by the second day, I was a physical mess.

And now I have my head in a red plastic bucket, heaving for all I'm worth. At least I'm not alone. Not everybody pukes the same way, though. I'm loud. I give it all I've got. The others find it funny to hear me. I throw up like I row: short on style but giving it 100 percent commitment.

After two days on the ocean, we learn that one type of food works better than others to minimize the suffering. People talk about ginger calming the stomach, but a little ginger cookie is not going to settle our guts when they reach such a state. We accept a certain degree of defeat and eat canned peaches. They taste exactly the same coming back up as they do going down in the first place. I particularly appreciate the way they pass back up the throat as effortlessly as they slip down.

At least it is possible for me to eat. Helen, on the other hand, cannot eat anything. Her digestive system still isn't normal. As a result, her energy levels nosedive. So Helen has stayed inside her cabin for a while, and she's missed a few turns at the oars. The rest of us are sympathetic. For now.

Like a normal boat, ours has a load of holes on deck—called scuppers—that allow water that crashes over us to drain away. Not being much of a sailor, I know nothing about how these scuppers work, and I completely freak out the first time that we get a truckload of ocean dumped over us. It's deep in the night as we enter rough waters. We've just taken a slapping from a particularly big wave, and I look down to see the deck has so much seawater on it that it looks as though I'm sitting in a bathtub. It must be a foot and a half high, and I stare at the water, expecting these drainage holes to do whatever they're supposed to do and get us back to normal. But nothing happens. As far as I can tell the water level on the deck is still as high as it was a few seconds ago. In that moment I realize there's a problem with the scuppers, and I conclude that since the water has no way to escape, we are—any second now—about to start sinking. Frozen, I am overwhelmed by fear. With great effort and in a feeble voice that I barely recognize as my own, I say to the other girls: "We're going down! We're going to drown!"

They don't share my sense of doom, and within a minute that feels like hours, the water has receded, and everyone on *The Guardian* is laughing hysterically, me included.

At other times I'm more in line with the feelings of others. Once when Kate and I are rowing we both burst into tears at the same time without saying anything beforehand. We try to keep rowing, and I have to admit that I feel embarrassed by the volume of my sobs and the quantity of my tears, but there's not a lot I can do to stop it.

"I'm happy to be here," I tell Kate, "but I never thought it would be so hard."

The sense of incredible vulnerability does it. I cannot escape by putting on a movie, going to the gym, or heading out and having a meal with someone else. I'm stuck here, about to face the hardest physical challenge of my life, and I have absolutely no means of escape. It feels so alien and so raw to be like this.

At some point during the first two days of the row—in between hurling peaches into the bucket, tipping them overboard, and washing it out—Debs comes out of the cabin, her face changed. I've seen the expression on her before. "I'm worried we're going too close to El Hierro."

I look up and see what she is talking about. To the south of us is the last of the Canary Islands, the last solid land we will see before reaching our final destination. Kate is meticulous about checking our course on deck, but we've had our heads down, battling the strong winds, concentrating on controlling the nausea, and trying to keep our oars from catching crabs—smacking a little too high into the water and slicing off just surface spray. We've not been paying attention to where we're going. Why should we? Isn't that what the Autohelm (which we've named Bertie) is supposed to be doing? We program in each of our twenty-one waypoints to the GPS, flip the switch, and let Bertie make all the adjustments to our rudder to make sure we're on course. Only right now, Bertie is not doing too well against the currents pushing us toward the rocky coastline of El Hierro.

Debs clambers into the empty rowing seat. She pulls hard on the oars, upping the pace, and her back strains beneath her jacket. A little of her anxiety starts to rub off on me, and I pull harder and faster to help battle the currents. It's dark now, and the lights of El Hierro look much closer than they did when Debs first came on deck. I can make out the car headlights driving along the cliff top and can see the whitecaps as they break on the rocks below. If we get dragged in too close and hit a submerged rock, even the smallest crack in our hull will finish us. We've only just begun, but this could be the end.

For the first time since we left, my fear is not about my ability to cope with the darkness or the sickness. I'm scared that we may not be able to trust this boat. All along I've assumed that it's a matter of our having the strength and the determination to keep going. As long as we work, we'll get there. Of course the weather will try to put us off, but when the storms hit we'll wait them out, then keep going to the very end.

Rowing outside Houses of Parliament, Anti-Slavery Day, October 18, 2011

Proud moment sharing our campaign with Prime Minister David Cameron

Sir Matthew Pinsent, naming our boat
The Guardian, Anti-Slavery Day, October 18, 2011

Deborah Paul

Training with Toby *(left)* Two years on and still rowing with my coach David *(right)*

Preparing our daily food packages

Brian Finke

Lots of tweaking and adjustments in La Gomera

All aboard! 3,000 miles ahead

Cabin life

I never tired of looking at this vast ocean

Always a relief to get through the night and watch the sunrise

Christmas Day, a hard day missing family but knowing this was a special one too

My rock and my rowing partner, Kate

Media interviews on the sat phone in a sweaty, hot cabin

Keep smiling through the rain

A glorious sunset, few and far between but breathtaking

Happy moments before arrival in Barbados

Celebration flares signal the end! We
spot Ross from the *Atlantic 4* and set
off our flares

Euphoria!

Brian Finke

Champagne arrival!

Brian Finke

Shattered, relieved, and joyful all at the same time

Brian Finke

Freedom Five—mission accomplished!

Brian Finke

First Finn to row the Atlantic

Stuart Tippleston

Jumping for joy the day after arrival
(Our legs still hurt!)

But what if *The Guardian* lets us down? What if this is one crossing too many for the old girl?

The crisis passes, and with Debs's help we pull away from land fairly quickly. Soon it's time to change over, and as I unstrap my foot leash and pivot my way back into the cabin, I take a last look at the island retreating behind us. It looks small already, too small to have been dangerous.

For some ocean rowers, the fear kicks in the moment they lose sight of land. We talked about this before we got on the water, and now we gently ask whether anyone's freaking out. But no one seems too worried about land disappearing from view—not that I have the energy to work out what the others are thinking and feeling.

Back in my cabin, I realize I'm exhausted. I've been tired before. I've been wiped out by a three-hour training session on the river, after working at my job that began at 4:00 a.m. I've been dizzy after going too many nights with too little sleep, waiting for Mum to be seen in a hospital. But this feeling goes way beyond what I have known. My hamstrings burn, my face stings from the constant assaults of the seawater, my head is numb from the concentration on all the vital tasks, and my hands have an ache so deep and painful that I can't imagine ever being able to straighten them out from this claw-like grip again. Even leaving the cabin feels like walking a tightrope, and the rowing takes so much mental energy I don't think I've noticed much of the sky or the sea.

Mostly I'm tired from the nights. I dread when the sun falls away and the darkness takes over. At home usually I'm full of life and excitement about going out when the lights come on. On the ocean I hate that fourteen hours must pass before the sky starts to lift behind us and the sun fights the shadows away. The lights around the boat help us see to move about, cook, and row, as well as to be seen by passing ships, but they're a feeble shield against the pitch-black a few feet beyond our oars. Our head flashlights aren't much better.

I close my eyes and try to remember what it is like to be at my home: the lights are on inside, and I look out a window to the lights of London beyond my door. I try to remember the times I've flown into Heathrow at night, peering down at the web of orange thread that covers the whole city, stretching farther than the tiny windows allow me to see. I try to remember the way the sky looks in the morning as the sun forces its way up from under the weight of the clouds. Before I can get more than a few seconds of each image, I am asleep.

"Teeeeeeen minutes!"

My sleep that seems to have lasted a few seconds is over. I open my eyes, and there's the darkness I've been trying to fight. Only now, it feels heavier, deeper, darker. The little light in my cabin is not working, and I have to get ready for my next watch by the light of my head flashlight.

I emerge to see the rest of the boat in darkness, with no deck lights shining. A small white guide light at the far end of the boat glimmers above my feet. I feel the fear. "What happened to the lights? Why are they off?"

"The battery tester's broken," explains Helen. "We can't tell how much power they're holding, and we can't run the risk of not having enough power to run the sat phone and the rest of the essential equipment."

We tested all the equipment before we left La Gomera, and everything was fine. I feel as powerless as I've ever felt in my whole life. Boat 0–Darkness 1.

My fear takes another bite out of me.

CHAPTER 15

These Waves Are . . .

I t's strange how comfortable my feet look when I row. They perch upon molded plastic ledges that hold them safely in place. Both footrests are lined with two layers of foam, a dense layer beneath a soft top layer. Each foot is strapped in carefully to provide the right balance between support and comfort. Too tight and the skin gets sore; too loose and my feet move about as I row.

We glued patches of sheepskin inside these foot straps, so they look like fluffy slippers, but they're difficult to get into. If the sheepskin slips during our watch, the harsh webbing of the foot straps can rub painfully against our skin. We must keep our bodies free from injury because we rely on all of our limbs out here.

As for the rest of our bodies, we sit on padded seats that we line with soft fleece towels. The seats move back and forth, pushed and pulled by our legs. They're the pistons that do most of the driving, while hands and arms concentrate on guiding the oar into the water just right, not so high as to catch a crab, not so deep as to leave the oar buried deep in the water.

Rowing places demands on almost every muscle in the body. Feet and ankles must constantly work to provide a stable base for the legs to work off. Calf muscles, thighs, hamstrings, and glutes push and pull with ceaseless regularity. Muscles around the abdomen and lower back must never switch off while the arms deal with eleven-foot-long oars weighing five pounds. We chose these oars that are longer and heavier than the oars of the other crews in the hope that the bigger oars will help us go faster. Already we're painfully aware that a rower needs the legs of a cyclist, the torso of a gymnast, and the arms of a swimmer.

Not all rowing is equal. Our cousins who slice up and down leafy rivers in their tiny boats that look like they've been designed with fighter jets in mind are a different breed. These flat-water rowers belong to the world of Ivy League colleges and perfect accents. All of us on *The Guardian* have spent time among them over the last year, but we don't belong there. I knew it from the moment I started training at a prestigious rowing club. As soon as I told them about the ocean rowing, they smiled, told me that was fascinating, and changed the subject. It's not that they were rude; it's more like the idea of rowing an ocean did not make sense to them. I might as well have told a sprinter I was going to run a marathon.

Flat-water rowing is all about perfection, power, and speed, especially when you're part of a crew. A fraction of an inch or a second either way, and you mess it up for everyone. It's about knowing what to do to get it right. No one screams on board a flat-water boat. There are no frantic fights for control.

Ocean rowing is different. Ocean rowers must battle the waves. If the flat-water crews are marked by grace, control, and perfection, we ocean rowers are all about guts and determination and the ability to keep going despite the chaos raging around us. If they're the thoroughbred racehorses, we're the Clydesdales. If they're performing a ballet, we're doing a Zumba workout.

Yet one thing is common to all rowers, no matter what type of water they're on. It's absolutely impossible to lie when you row. You can't cover up the truth about the condition of your body when you're on a boat. Not had enough sleep? It'll show. Not eaten properly? It'll show. Not fully confident that you can make it? Everybody's going to know it. From the rhythm of your oars to the amount of miles tracked by the GPS, you cannot lie when you row.

I should be the one struggling right now. Out of the five of us on board, I'm definitely the least prepared. Debs and Katie did a twenty-four-hour row together in Dubai some months ago, and before Kate flew to La Gomera she was setting her alarm to wake up at 2:00 a.m. so that she could spend a couple of hours on her rowing machine. There's no way I was going to be able to get close to that kind of preparation. The past few months with the logistics of the row, the hunt for sponsors, and Mum's struggles at home, I have been hanging on by my fingernails. More than a few times I've said that I was looking forward to getting onto *The Guardian* for a rest. I thought I could find peace on the water.

Although the other girls are better prepared, some are struggling more than I am. Helen's seasickness has been bad since the beginning, but as another day passes without her eating much of anything, she has spent a lot of time in the cabin. Now, five days in, Debs is in trouble.

"Look at this," she says as she pulls down her shorts and bends over.

"Woah!" I say, more than a little shocked by the intimacy, but my discomfort is immediately forgotten when I take a closer look. Her backside looks awful. It's covered in red sores, like a pizza loaded with pepperoni. "Ouch."

She's a tough girl, but she's holding back tears as she describes the pain. Even with the two foam seat pads, our backsides are being severely punished. The combination of friction, pressure, and seawater—and our inability to get fully clean or dry in our tiny cabins—means that it was only a matter of time before one of us had an infection there.

"You can't row like this, Debs," Helen says.

"But I don't want to stop," she says.

Just as we responded to Helen's plight, we're all sympathetic, but we know that for the time Debs is out of action we're pulling her across the ocean. "We know that, Debs," I say. "But it's in everyone's best interest for you to wait for the antibiotics to kick in and deal with whatever bacteria are having a party on your body."

Begrudgingly, she agrees. "But only if I take over the job of boiling up all the water and preparing all our meals."

I'm glad she does because I begin to figure out why I've been so exhausted. Up to now I've eaten only breakfast, lunch, and dinner, sticking to a normal daily routine on land. But with Debs constantly asking whether people want a meal, I realize that the others have been eating far more often than I have. Doing that makes sense since there is no difference between night and day in our endless cycle of rowing and resting. The three-hour shifts that we tried for the first few nights are just too long, even though the extra sleep is heavenly. Now we swap every two hours, day and night. When I eat something during most breaks, I start to feel a whole lot better—or at least a whole lot less terrible.

Despite everything, we laugh. We need laughter more than ever. From time to time someone shouts out, "Whose freaking idea was this?" I grin and shrug my shoulders every time. "Sorry, girls!"

Back home, my main experience of the ocean was from the beach. There I'd watch the waves form an orderly line and approach the shore from the same direction. Out here, there are no rules for the waves. When I row, without any warning at all a wave can spring up from the side and force the oar up, sending my hands and the thick bit of wood they're grasping violently down, scraping all the way along my shins.

Every once in a while the boat will be thrown into a fizz of adrenaline by the sound of someone screaming in pain. We'll ask if the rower is okay, and the usual reply comes through clenched teeth: "Shins!" Our oars are so heavy and the waves so fierce that when they smash into our legs, the pain is intense. Long before the bruising has time to heal, the thin layer of skin takes another bashing. And then another.

For someone like me who wants to be in control, the hardest part of this whole experience is impotence. I can eat well to try to keep up my energy levels, and I can clean the salt off my body with baby wipes every time I crawl back into the cabin—even though I'm so exhausted all I want to do is fall asleep in my foul weather gear, and I often do. It's easier to collapse in my salty, damp padded outfit that makes me look like I belong on a shipping trawler than to spend the precious minutes staying awake and wriggling out of it.

I can make sure that my feet are strapped in and my hand pads are properly fitted between my raw-looking palms and my oars. But preparation and care can get me only so far. If the waves decide to smash my oars onto my legs, they will. If they decide to rattle me in my windowless cabin so hard that I throw up, they will. If these thirty- and forty-foot waves as tall as a house decide to capsize us, they will.

We're powerless on this powerful ocean. Sometimes, all I can do is try to hide from the waves in my cabin and pray. I've prayed on and off over my life, starting as a young child thanking God for pretty dresses and flowers. Like many people, I got out of the habit as I became a teenager, but as the complications and heartbreaks of adult life presented themselves, I often wanted to talk to someone. Since God had never given me bad advice, I started talking to him again whenever things were messy. I don't use fancy words, and I don't have to sit in a church. I mainly get in my car, turn off the radio, and say whatever's on my mind as I drive. I talk to God as if he sits next to me. I get angry, and sometimes I shout and even swear. I don't think he stops listening. And when I have nothing else to say, I stop. In the silence I feel better. Something has calmed within me. Those times are amazing.

I pray a lot out here on the ocean. I pray a lot on land, too, but among the wind and the waves, it feels as though the words matter more. Does God answer every single one of my requests in the way I want? Of course not, but I've never regarded prayer as a coin to be put in a divine vending machine. So why do I pray? I pray because I believe that there are so many ways in which it works. It helps me have a clearer perspective. It calms me down. It reminds me why I'm here. And sometimes I think it changes things.

Here on the boat I pray that God will give me the strength to get through this, and if not that, at least the right conditions to get us across. Sometimes I lie here and cry when I should be eating or sleeping or cleaning myself up. The tears help until another wave jolts me sideways and reminds me that whatever the waves want to do, they will do.

CHAPTER 16

Rope and Glue

Bertie the Autohelm wasn't entirely innocent when we were pushed dangerously close to El Hierro. We all wanted to give him the benefit of the doubt, but as of five minutes ago it's perfectly clear that he's struggling. It's day six, and we're already down by two vital pieces of equipment. I shudder to think what state we'll be in by the time we make it across. *If* we make it across.

The Autohelm is a great invention. It is a simple device that sits on the side of the boat, extending or retracting its metal arm to continually make adjustments to the ropes connected to the rudder underneath. Linked to our GPS, it should quietly make sure we are headed precisely where we need to go. Okay, perhaps not quietly; we've grown used to the continual buzz and whirr that it emits as it tweaks our course. It's comforting to hear.

But right now the noise is anything but comforting. The solid sounds of gentle steering have been joined by new ones—a pop and a low grinding noise. Each time it tells us that Bertie has broken away from the boat, losing contact with the rudder.

To make matters worse, it's nighttime. Maybe we should wait, but if we don't fix it now we run the risk of rowing off course and

wasting time we don't have. The waves are doing their best to tor-
ment us, throwing spray over the deck with plenty of force, and
there's no moon to work by. We want to have enough battery left
for emergency calls we might have to make, so we don't turn on the
deck lights. Kate and Debs have on their head flashlights, and they
are trying to fix Bertie. They have marine glue—an industrial-
strength waterproof adhesive—washers, nuts, and a load of rope.

It's like we're in a movie, with the waves attacking us as we
battle to keep going. Every time they manage to get Bertie to stay
in place and we take off, he soon pops out again. Eventually someone calls it. Bertie's giving up. He's not going to make it.

There's always a backup, and with Bertie gone, we switch to
foot steering. The person sitting in the middle of the three rowing seats has to use her right foot to adjust the pulley system that
controls the rudder, and to do that she has to constantly check the
GPS screen on deck, the compass, and the weather bird (a kind of
weather vane that we named Peter). It's a daunting task in and of
itself. Add the stress and strain of keeping her oars going well, dealing with nausea, and the acts of random violence when the ocean
overrules her oars and uses them to attack her shins, and life for
her is a lot harder.

Thankfully Kate's brilliant at it, and whenever we row, she's
the best at keeping us on course. The extra effort is taking its toll,
and in the same way that the oars become the ocean's weapons, so
the boat around the steering area smacks her ankles. The flickering
screen confirms that our little pink line has remained as straight
and true as it ever was. Yet after a few nights she is exhausted. An
old hockey injury—a broken knee—acts up, so I take charge of
keeping us on course. But I'm completely awful at the task, not to
mention I lack Kate's patience and precision.

The loss of Bertie gets me thinking. We took a course in ocean survival and celestial navigation so we would know how to navigate by the sun, the moon, and the stars. We learned how to drag a body through and out of the water and back into a boat. We learned what to do if someone died while on board, how to use the body bag in a way that would minimize the health risk to the rest of us. We learned the theory of how to survive on the life raft, relying on the highly calorific emergency rations that looked like chalk.

Any number of things could lead us headfirst into a disaster. If we do get in trouble, we can call *Aurora* to come to our rescue. But because she's going to be out here on the waves until the last crew lands in Barbados, we could spend three or four months on her. The idea of failing at the race and being forced to watch it eke out in slow motion to the very end is unpleasant in the extreme. Of course, maritime law says that whoever's nearest to a distress call will go to the boat's aid, so if we get in real trouble there's a chance that we might get picked up by a fast-moving tanker. Who knows where we'd end up then?

The prospect of coming close to a container ship is a very real concern to all of us. There are no shipping lanes on the Atlantic, which means that the whole ocean is one big fast-lane highway without anyone patrolling. The only rule is that the biggest and fastest vessels get their way, so a tiny vessel like ours must keep an eye out for danger and make sure that we're far enough away.

Some container ships are so large—up to twelve hundred feet long—and go so fast—twenty-five knots (almost twenty-nine miles) per hour—that in rough seas there's no chance of their seeing us.[1]

Early on I mess up in keeping a watchful eye on the water. Since Katie and I sit at the bow, it's up to whichever of us is rowing to avoid coming too close to anything on the ocean. The plan is to look around, over our shoulders, every fifteen minutes or so, but I'm too busy concentrating on my rowing to pay attention to anything else. Nobody is pleased with me when suddenly, completely out of nowhere, we're about sixty feet from a huge fishing boat. We've not seen any boats after losing sight of land, so I suppose I'm really not expecting to almost crash into something like this. But as soon as it arrives, it disappears. Despite the adrenaline surge, I feel a little sad once it slips from view.

The same thing happens later in the row. I'm rowing and supposed to be watching the equipment, as well as the ocean, but not doing a good job of it. We close in on a mammoth container ship. The GPS tells us that it's carrying dangerous goods, and it's about five miles away. Five miles might seem like a long way, but one of these moving metal islands can't stop on a dime. Besides, these guys have a deadline to hit and a profit to make, so there's no way that they're going to stop for a little rowing boat like ours. It's up to us to keep out of their way and let them know we're here.

Debs tries reaching them on the radio, but there's no reply at first. She persists until, with limited English-speaking skills, they answer. She is able to get the message across, and they pass ahead of us without making fatal last-minute course changes. But I learn a vital lesson. Again.

Container ships can be dangerous for us, yet getting hit by them does not worry us the most. We're far more concerned about a floating container beneath the surface striking *The Guardian*. There are between five and six million containers being transported on the world's oceans at any one time, and the violence of the storms means that every year some of them work loose and fall into the ocean. The percentage of containers that jump ship is tiny (0.005 percent), but insurers estimate that as many as two thousand containers are lost at sea each year.[2] You wouldn't think that these twenty-foot-long metal boxes would float, but they're well sealed and some of them can float for a while before sinking. Even the slightest glance from one can tear a hole in a boat like ours.

Everything fits into the rhythm of our 120-minute shifts—sleeping, rowing, eating, washing, puking, pooing, cleaning ourselves up, and even conversing. When one watch ends, every task on the boat ceases, and limbs clamber over each other as oars are grabbed and stowed and rowers replaced with the shortest pause possible. If it takes a minute longer than it should when we change, those twelve minutes of lost rowing time will soon add up. After fifty days we will have wasted ten hours bobbing on the ocean.

These changeovers matter, and we don't stop unless absolutely necessary. We had to pause for a few hours, when Bertie died, to set up the foot steering. We were rowing as soon as we could. We realize how bad it is when, on day ten, we're rowing and suddenly feel the hull—the underside—of the boat shudder.

"Oh," says Kate. "Oh, no. It's broken. The foot steering's broken."

CHAPTER 17

Prayers to Michael

When we can't row, we're at the mercy of the winds. So we are supposed to deploy our parachute anchor, a nine-foot-wide parachute that is let out on a long line behind the boat. It acts like an airborne parachute and slows the progress, pulling the boat along with the current instead of the wind. It's a simple idea, but getting it out of the hatch, setting it up, and deploying it in exactly the right way takes practice. We should have practiced this operation on land and in the marina's calm waters many times. But we didn't.

Having heard from other rowers how hard it can be to deploy one, my safety-conscious sister kept reminding me to get the parachute anchor out while we were in La Gomera. We tried to use it one time in the hurried rush of the final two days before we set off, but the lesson didn't sink in. How I wish I'd listened to her!

She was right about other things too. Joy bought me a hat and gloves, warning me about the cold. I begrudgingly took the hat but ditched the gloves, and again I regret not listening to her. I've had a rotten cold and violent sore throat over the last few days, and having a pair of gloves in the cabin would be so wonderful.

We don't have a clue how to use the parachute anchor, but it may not make a lot of difference to us as we sit here. The winds are being kind, and I don't think we're drifting too far off course. Not like Samuelsen and Harbo in the *Fox*. One storm was so severe that they couldn't row. They had to wait for it to pass, and by the time it did, they had drifted twenty miles back toward New York.[1]

We've been fortunate so far. Only one time during the twelve days that have passed since we left La Gomera have the wind and the waves been so strong that we have given up rowing. We all squeezed into the cabins, and the chance of getting a few hours of extra sleep was appealing. Katie was soon snoring, but I was in no state to relax. The air became claustrophobic, and I started to panic. My face was pressed up to the hull, I was wringing wet, and it was pitch-black. I felt hemmed in from all sides but was too tired to cry. Fear took over. The hatch door steamed up, and I kept opening it a little to gulp in fresh air. Those were some of the longest hours of my life.

Even then we didn't deploy the parachute anchor because Peter the bird told us that the winds were pushing us in the right direction. Later, we found out that other crews did not have such good luck. Some deployed their parachute anchors, and their rudders broke under the force of the waves.

After much effort and plenty of skill, Helen and Debs bolt the foot steering together again, this time using such a massive amount of nuts, bolts, washers, and rope that I doubt it will come loose again. As I watch them work I realize I don't know the difference between a washer and a nut, and I don't think I've ever used an adjustable wrench in my life. This world on the ocean is nothing like what I thought it would be. Still, we're underway after two hours, our race across the Atlantic unpaused and set to play again.

That is, until the next thing goes wrong. Katie and I have the job of making sure that the boat's weight is equally balanced at all times. We packed all our food into the twelve storage hatches spread around the deck, and we drew a detailed map of what can be found where. When we take out the daily rations for each person, we ensure that each hatch contains an equal weight.

I might not have done so well at watching out for land or container ships, but I take my job as packing supervisor very seriously. I know where everything is, and I know how the boat should feel when she's properly balanced. The slightest shift is enough to make me reevaluate the situation. So when I wake up one day and find that I've pretty much rolled all the way to one side, I know something is seriously wrong.

Checking the hatches on the side that is listing over, I am horrified to see a massive amount of water inside. The packs of food—all wrapped in plastic and packing tape and labeled with the person's initials and the packs' contents—float about like apples in a barrel.

"Girls," I say. "We've got a problem." They stare as Kate and I solemnly remove the waterlogged packages from the hatches. Everyone's concerned.

"How bad is it?"

"How much have we lost?"

"I don't know," I say. We won't know how serious it is until we've done a full inventory. Others bail water while I check what was affected. I grab the knife attached to the deck and slice open the packages. It's a massive job, and we end up spending days of time when we're not rowing sorting through the supplies and rebagging what's left. Most of our chocolate snacks are inedible, which is terrible news considering that I didn't start taking my birth control pills early enough and I'm having a period that has lasted these first twelve days of the journey. In all the craziness of the final days I forgot to pack any pain relief. And I could really do with chocolate right now. Even worse, all of Kate's dairy-free food is ruined. Everything left to eat will seriously mess up her digestive system.

I've been trying hard to be brave, but I'm genuinely worried that we won't make it. For the first time since planning this adventure two years ago, I seriously contemplate the prospect of our failure. I've imagined we might not quite break the record, and that brings on cold sweats and makes me work harder whenever I'm next at the oars. But I've never thought we would fail completely. The very thought of failure makes my stomach contract.

After bailing out the hatches, we can see the problem. The holes that we tried to patch up with marine glue before we departed are back with a vengeance. We try to use the glue again without success. We decide to call Simon and ask for his help. Five girls in a leaky boat in the middle of the Atlantic, and we have to call a man to help us get out of this mess. The humiliation is trumped only by the fear of sinking. And the fear is very real. The waves pick up again, the light fades, and we start to drift around so that we're sitting side on (*beam on*) to the waves. If a big enough one comes along and catches us sitting right across it, there's a real risk of capsizing.

Overwhelmed, Kate is crying. Debs is in the cabin, making the call, and Katie is in our cabin. Helen and I try to work with the parachute anchor, but the jumbled mess of fabric seems impossible to sort out. The waves continually knock us off balance, and I often check that my foot leash is firmly attached at both ends. My mind goes back to a conversation I had with an ex–ocean rower. "When you feel the boat starting to flip, take deep breaths, protect your head as you enter the water, and keep your eyes open. You'll spin and be disoriented, but you'll be okay as long as you stay calm. Once you surface, count the number of other heads you can see above water, say your name, and announce your status. Stay calm. Remember to control your breathing."

Simon's reaction is disappointing. I don't know what I expected from him. Maybe an apology, maybe sympathy or a tone of concern in his voice. When Debs emerges from the cabin she repeats word for word what he said: "Welcome to ocean rowing, girls! Welcome to ocean rowing."

At the time I find his response annoying. Later I'll see that he's right. I'll understand that this is a journey where we have to learn to fix our problems.

I usually try to stay positive, and I'll always find a way to get enthusiastic about something. Even if the glass is cracked and dirty, and contains a single drop of water, I'll believe that it's on the way to being full. But now I feel about as low as I've ever felt.

Even the most basic daily tasks get me down. There are ways of doing things on a boat, and following the proper steps matters. Like doing a poo. We call the technique "bucket and chuck it." It involves carefully lowering the poo-laden bucket into the water to empty it of its contents, then scooping up seawater to rinse it properly. Early on I completely mess up when I allow far too much water to get into the bucket, feel the weight increase, and watch as one of our key toilets disappears into the ocean. Debs looks at me, horrified, which is about as bad as I feel. Thankfully we have a spare bucket that we tie securely to the boat in order to keep our bathroom facilities working at full capacity.

Things start to feel a little better as we settle into the row. The seasickness has passed for all of us except Helen, who's still struggling. We respect her for soldiering on when she clearly feels awful.

I'm in the cabin, just dozing, when I hear a commotion outside and peek out to investigate.

I see Debs turn round to face me, her eyes wide. "The watermaker caught fire!"

I see a whiff of smoke coming out of the cabin behind her. She sits down and explains. "I got to it just after it started. It's out now, but it won't work anymore. The electrics are all shot."

The watermaker is essential to our survival; it desalinates around six liters (or 1.3 gallons) an hour, enough to keep us hydrated throughout the day. After the smoke clears, we can tell that the hatch where it is located has a leak, and that caused the overheating and failure of the watermaker. We swallow our pride and call Jim, whose number we have been given and told to call if the watermaker goes wrong. He explains that the problem can probably be fixed with a fuse. Would you believe it? We don't have any spares. We don't even have fuses we can take out of something else. Our friends on the *Atlantic 4* are ahead of us, and they offer to stop and let us catch up so that they can give us one of their spare fuses, but we can't accept. If we do, our crossing will have been supported, and we will be disqualified from any world record we might set. We thank them for the kind offer, but we struggle on by ourselves.

Jim tries to think of other ways to fix the machine, but the result is the same. We have no way of making drinking water automatically. Our best hope lies in bailing out the hatch and waiting a few days in the hope that it will miraculously fix itself, but it's every bit as dead when it's dry as when it's wet.

Kate and I pray every kind of prayer that we can think of. Our faith is childlike, and our optimism is high. We believe that there's going to be a genuine resurrection right here on this boat, but our watermaker shows no sign of life.

I've opened a few letters from friends and family, and they've often helped. With the death of the watermaker I decide to open another. The one from my boss catches my eye. She's a devout Catholic, and though we never talk much about religion, I admire the way she carries what she believes. It's like an anchor for her, keeping her steady no matter what the storms are doing around her. She wrote, "When I was young my grandma used to always say, 'If ever something electrical goes wrong, pray to St. Michael—the patron saint of radiologists and paramedics.' You should remember that."

I couldn't have asked for a clearer sign. I tell the rest of the girls about the letter. All of us—two atheists, one agnostic, and a couple of enthusiastic Christians—start praying:

"Michael! Hey, Michael! Help us, would you?"

"Michael, we need you to fix our watermaker, okay?"

"Come on, Michael, you know you want to!"

"Fix it! Fix it! Fix it, Michael!"

We laugh and shout for all we're worth:

"Please, Michael. Can you fix it? Thanks. And amen."

He doesn't, by the way.

CHAPTER 18

It Gets Personal

A fter two weeks on the ocean, each of us is starting to show the signs of the physical stress the row is placing us under. Our fingers are bent around like claws, unable to straighten out. Our skin is puffy, red, and cracked. Our nails are ripped, tender, and bruised. I don't recognize these hands, but I know they are mine. I can feel the pain in them as I try to flex my fingers.

My hands are not the only part of me changing on this row. I hear myself say things that sound as painful and ugly as my hands look. Some people say that stress causes individuals to show their most honest, least filtered versions of themselves. If that's true, my current version is not one that I like. Over the past few days I have screamed in anger, sobbed in fear as I curled up with my little wooden cross in the cabin, and felt unable to go on. The one constant is that my heart rate rises when the stress increases.

The stress and strain affect all of us. Too much rowing, not enough sleeping, too little drinking, and too many days puking have physically drained us. We're emotionally spent from living with the constant calculations about how far we've gone, how likely we are to break the record, and how close we've come to total disasters.

Each of us reacts to stress in different ways. Kate becomes quiet and withdraws a little while Debs somehow manages to laugh when things get tough. Katie is most like me and changes depending on her mood. Helen lets it all out, and we are surprised that she can swear like a real sailor. Cussing and raging at the machines as they break down are not helpful, but what can we do? It is the way she seems to cope.

We finally have to admit that the watermaker is beyond resurrection. *The Guardian*—like the *Fox*, that very first ocean rowing boat—does contain big, floodable ballast tanks of water, designed to help us flip back over if we capsize. Hand-pumping the ocean water in and out is a time-consuming task. And we're not allowed to drink the fifty liters of freshwater ballast we're carrying unless we have an emergency and the handpumping fails. So we get out the handheld water desalinator, which we call Viv (short for Viv Evian, another great name that came out of having so much time on our hands). Viv looks like a cross between a large bicycle pump and a long-arm stapler. It has various tubes coming in and out of it, and if you put them in the right places and pump your arm up and down slowly for an hour, you can produce enough drinking water to keep one of us hydrated for a day—about a gallon.

There are just two problems. First, the pumping adds a new task to an already overworked crew. Someone could pump instead of row, but that will only slow us down. We decide that everyone will take turns sitting in the vacant third rowing seat (which is also broken and completely unfixable) and pumping water while Kate and I row. It means less rest and more strain on our already tired muscles, but it's the best choice. We try to inject a little fun into it, and Katie is crowned Water Pump Queen, having nailed the technique so perfectly that she can produce more water than the rest of us.

The other problem is the water itself. The drinking water produced by the hand pump doesn't taste like the water made by the machine. We have trouble getting used to it, and just when we get over the seasickness, we reach for the puke buckets again as our stomachs revolt against this new liquid. And, because we do not hold it down, we risk dehydration again, which means having to pump more drinking water. We are locked in a vicious, salty cycle.

Early on in the days of pumping the stress gets to me, and I am about to erupt with rage. My nausea is strong, I'm dehydrated, and I have a banging headache. If I remembered to bring my personal medical kit I'd have the painkillers to relieve what's going on in my skull. But I didn't bring the pills, and even though I've borrowed some from Katie, her supplies are low. So I hold back on the quantity I'd usually take. I complain about the hand pump making my arm sore, and I'm one millisecond away from losing it. Then I hear Debs say, "Well, that's just how it is, all right?"

I've had it. I slam down the water bottle that I've been filling, get to my knees, and scream at her: "I don't give a crap about these world records. If we need to use that ballast water, we're using it. I don't care what you say. This isn't 'just how it is.' I'm not pumping anymore."

"No, Julia," says Debs. "That's not what I said. I said, 'It's going to be all right.'"

Oh. I exhale and take my seat again.

Thankfully others have been here before, and we've been sent on our way with good advice. One friend of mine, Margaret Bowling, has rowed the Atlantic twice. Two things she told me have stayed with me throughout: "Whenever you are out of the cabin, you must be sure that your foot leash is attached. Getting swept overboard is by far the biggest risk facing an ocean rower. Never forget that you risk death daily, and you must never, ever become complacent. It needn't take a massive wave to slap any one of you off the boat, and there are plenty of big waves. If it did happen, the chances of being able to stop the boat and get back in time to the person overboard are slim, even without twenty-foot waves and high winds."

One day, when there's no real wind to speak of and the rowing is particularly tough going, Helen stares out at the water. "I'm desperate to get in there," she says. "Besides, someone's got to remove those barnacles attached to the boat. They're probably slowing us down a bit."

So we get Helen in a harness and keep a firm grip as she enters the water. We row while she cleans the boat, and we're shocked at how far back she drifts within seconds of jumping in, even though we feel as though we're rowing through molasses.

"Don't ever think we're not moving fast, girls," she says after she catches up with us. "There's no way on earth I'd be able to get back if the wind was up."

The second valuable piece of advice from Margaret was about conflict. She told me, "Julia, you just have to let things go. When you're feeling angry with someone, ask yourself this: will it still matter in two years?"

The longer the row lasts the more chances I have to practice this technique. Increasingly the others annoy me. Sometimes at night when I try to sleep for an hour or so, Helen and Katie sing their lungs out. I lie in the cabin, eyes wide open, reminding myself of Margaret's words. Sometimes it works, and I calm down; other times the temptation to yell out to them to keep it down is too hard to resist.

The first signs of conflict start to show. Sometimes it's between me and Debs or me and Helen. Katie and Kate are so beautifully laid-back that they seem immune to the strain. But not me. I can't always swallow my frustrations.

The main area of conflict is the satellite phone and the ways in which we use it. We agree that it will be best not to phone home often because we will remember all the things that we miss. But we do use the phone to keep in touch with media, sponsors, and supporters. The thing is, most of those key people are contacts that I've built up over the last year or so. Because my sister is probably the most amazing PR machine any crew could hope for, she works crazily hard at home to build the buzz about the row. When we have a story to tell, it's just as likely that we'll send a text to my sister as to the PR company we hired.

Deborah—a friend back home—provides information to all the churches supporting us. And because many of my church friends and their contacts have enabled us to raise much of our money and build a network of supporters who share our story on social media—as well as get on their knees to pray when things go wrong—I need to keep in touch with Deborah on a fairly regular basis. Through Joy and Deborah, I get to have the forbidden fruit of contact with home.

CHAPTER 19

Something to Row For

It must be day sixteen, or thereabouts, when I notice that the sky is darker than usual this night. There's no moon to guide us, only the dim bulb of the navigation light. There's no glorious light show sent to earth by nameless stars and galaxies a billion miles away. Instead there's just a vast ink-black ocean that bleeds into a vast ink-black sky.

My hands are sore, and my bones cry out for sleep. Yet my body knows that there is no chance of picking my way out of this seat before my two hours are up. I'm held here by the invisible chains of the task that we have set ourselves. All I can do is row and wait for the next wave to land on me. Back and forth I slide on this tiny seat, my legs, arms, and back pushing and pulling, my eyes blinking back the saltwater. Sometimes I can't tell whether these are my tears or the ocean water running down my face.

Even though there are so many times when I wonder why I do this, it's not long before I remember. Her name is Alejandra.

I met her in an airport. I was flying out, she was flying in, and our mutual friend was adamant that we should meet. I needed to hear Alejandra's story, she said. It would change my life forever.

Alejandra was—is—beautiful. She's from Mexico City and has the olive skin and dark hair that hold a certain mystery for a blonde girl from Finland like me. We sat in the café, surrounded by the typical chaos of the airport, and she told me what happened to her. She cried as she spoke. We both did.

She was eighteen when someone told her about a job available north of the city. She traveled up there, but it was a lie. She was trapped, sold, and shipped out to the highest bidder. For the next five years she was forced to work as a prostitute, moved from brothel to brothel as one owner traded her for another. She became like livestock, her body seen only as a means of creating a profit for whoever fenced her into her tiny room.

Twenty, thirty times a day men visited her. Her pimp beat her, others urinated on her, and one pimp threw scorpions on her, all the time trying to degrade her and break her down. Pimps don't want a human spirit alive within the body. They can't sell that. They want the flesh just alive enough to move but not strong enough to fight.

When there were no more words left to say, and I could no longer ignore the final boarding calls for my flight, we parted. "I'm going to do the row for you, Alejandra," I said. Alejandra said nothing at first, but took off her earrings. As she put them in my hands, she smiled.

"Keep them and remember me, Julia."

I sobbed all the way to America.

Other faces come to me when I row or rest. I can see the eyes of Elena, a girl I met when I visited a safe house in Greece that was run by my friends at the A21 Campaign. She was rescued the day before from a brothel and brought to their safe house. After months of being tricked, traded, and abused by men, she was finally safe, but her eyes told the story of where she had been. There was no life in them.

I've met girls whose parents sold them because they were too poor to eat; they fell for the lies of the traffickers who promised to offer well-paying jobs to the girls. I've met girls who were captured against their will. I've met girls who were trapped by strangers, and others who were betrayed and imprisoned by the very people who once declared that they loved them. I've met girls from different countries, including Mexico, China, Nigeria, Romania, and even a British girl, born and bred in England. All of these girls are unique. Some are beautiful, some are not, but all have one thing in common: they could have been me.

As I row, I remember the facts too. An estimated thirty million people are trapped in slavery today.[1] Men, women, and children are forced to work as manual and sexual laborers against their will. The average age of a trafficking victim is twelve to fourteen years old.[2] Every thirty seconds someone new is trapped and forced into the bondage of modern slavery.[3]

That's why I row. It's why we all row. When it hurts, I take thirty more strokes to remember the thirty million. My elbows are inflamed, my hamstrings are screaming, and my wrists are bruised from the weight of the oars and repetition of hauling them back and forth. As I take thirty more strokes I think, *Would it be worse to have someone rape me forty times a day or to put up with this discomfort a while longer?* My pain pales into insignificance.

These physical challenges are bad enough, but the mental battle is the fiercest and brings the biggest challenges. Thinking of the 3,000 miles that we have to row is so overwhelming that I make it slightly less daunting by taking it watch by watch: *All*

I need to do is these two hours. Get these done, Julia. That's all you have to do.

This challenge is changing me. The gift of perspective is wonderful. When life is stripped of everything that doesn't matter, I can see more clearly. I think about what I want in life, what I want to spend myself on, what I want to achieve, and who I want to be. I don't have all the answers yet, but bit by bit, I'm headed in the right direction.

I'm used to picking myself up when things are tough, but this is nothing like taking part in a running race or failing to finish in the top three at a school athletics meet. I've faced brick walls, but they have not been as thick or as high as the ones I face out here. But I'm learning how to get through them. I need to preach to myself, to pick up my mental attitude and not let negative thoughts get in the way. I'm learning that if I believe everything that I say I believe about God, I should be able to endure this discomfort, battle the self-doubt and fear, and expect good to emerge.

So many times when I was back on land I thought I had made good progress, only to be dragged back again by the same old junk. Good things happened, then I remembered the old wounds—the pain of everything that happened at home, the fear about what will happen to Mum, the anger of being caught in a relationship with someone who brought out the absolute worst in me. I struggled to break free of all this, but here on the boat I'm getting a new perspective on my life. I can see that if I can push through at home the way I'm learning to push through out here, surely everything will be a little bit different.

But it's not all black and white. From the start Kate and I agree to pray for the thirty million as we row at night. She has such a gentle voice that the wind often whips her words away. It's a reminder of the problem at the heart of what we're doing. How can we hope to make a difference? Aren't our actions too small, just as our prayers are too weak for the wind?

I've met British girls, exploited in the UK, and other girls who were trafficked into the UK. The truth is that for the ones who are rescued, the past rarely goes away. They must live with the knowledge that some people really cannot be trusted, that bad things do happen to good people, and that the very resilience they relied on while they were raped by strangers is going to be required to get them through the rest of their lives. It's a burden that lasts a lifetime, one we can never fully lift from their shoulders. But what we can do is restore their hope.

We pray for the victims of trafficking to find the resilience to get through it. I wish we could pray for fairy-tale endings, but the world of human trafficking and prostitution does not share the same script as *Pretty Woman*. There is no fairy godmother who can wave her wand and free the slave, instantly releasing her from the pain of her suffering. It takes time and strength. It takes the ability to endure the struggles as they continue to bite until, one day, they fade far enough away.

Resilience. Fortitude. We rarely hear these words today, but they're hidden gems of the human soul. We need more of them; I need more of them, even though I am just beginning to see that these traits can be formed only through struggle and difficulty.

If I am to become the strong woman I believe I can be, I'm going to have to fight for it—not against others, but against the doubt and impatience that bubble up within me.

CHAPTER 20

The Gamble

I wake up, immediately aware that something's different. I run through the possibilities. Is the boat listing? No. Am I injured? No. Can I hear anything unusual, like a tanker in the distance or a piece of our remaining equipment starting to malfunction? No. Gradually, the mist clears in my mind. I feel fine. For the first time since we left I was not soaked to the skin when I crawled into the cabin at the end of the last watch. For the first time, Kate and I felt as though we had momentum as we rowed. And right now, I'm not cold.

Even though we were wearing shorts, T-shirts, and flip-flops in La Gomera, I've been shivering pretty much since we lost sight of land. I never thought about the cold. After all, I saw photos of crews wearing barely any clothes. Staying dry was a concern, however. Like the other girls, I have an expensive sailing jacket and salopettes, which keep out most of the spray but are useless when a wave lands on me. They're not much good at keeping out the cold. None of us brought gloves.

If we drop farther south, we'll be back in T-shirts and shorts in no time. Down there—where all the other crews can be found—the air is warmer, the hoped-for waves are bigger, and the winds are stronger. They hope to catch the southerly trade winds and get turbo boosted across the ocean, just like the old sailing ships in the days when these waters transported human souls by the boatload. But we're staying up here, taking the shortest, most direct route across the Atlantic to get to Barbados. We're taking a gamble, but isn't everyone? Yes, there's a chance that those crews to the south of us could catch the good winds, but they also risk forty- and fifty-foot waves and the chaos they can bring. Our gamble might just pay off.

Everything's a paradox. The big waves leave us physically and emotionally exhausted, particularly when they prowl around the boat at night, out of sight, pouncing at random and leaving us wet and fearful. But they give us power as well, adding vital speed to our crossing. We fear them, and many times I pray for the waves to stop. Yet when they're gone and the waters are flatter, our daily progress drops off. Soon I pray for the big weather to return.

It's around this time that we receive a message from the organizers that we are on the edge of a patch of good weather—meaning big waves and high winds, a basic nightmare for anyone other than a crazed bunch of ocean rowers desperate to pick up speed. The GPS screen shows our progress, and our PR company and the race organizers inform us that our hard work has been paying off. We have refused to stop for anything but the most severe problems. We have chased every single moment to try to smash the current fifty-day record, pulling hard on the oars and loving it whenever a text reports our ever-improving race position. The boat erupts with whoops and cheers as we picture ourselves chasing down the pack. We were the underdogs, but going out two days later than everyone else gave us more motivation to hunt them down. Nothing spurs us on quite as much as hearing that we're overtaking crews or that we covered the most mileage the day before.

We've had our eyes on another crew, *Atlantic Dash*. Happy amateurs like us, both of them are firefighters. They loaded their boat with enough booze to keep a submarine crew happy for a month, and we've been level with them the last few days. At times as little as five miles separate us, putting them just over the horizon. The next few days as we wait for the big weather to catch us and slingshot us farther ahead, *Atlantic Dash* streaks ahead of us. They get the boost while we must be stuck in a pocket of too little pressure, sitting solidly beneath gray skies, on flat seas with oars that feel as though they are full of holes.

As this truth sinks deeper into our minds, I notice a change. We still battle beneath the same sunless skies, but the mood lightens. We emerge from our personal skirmishes with fear, exhaustion, infected backsides, and whatever else is troubling us, and we start to enjoy the experience.

I am so used to this new daily routine that it hardly strikes me as odd that sometimes before a watch I'll open the hatch doorway and see Kate coming out, totally nude, laughing and screaming, "Naked woman!"

Since the weather has broken and the sun reappears, we've decided to strip off and row naked. It's not about getting a tan or looking alluring. No other people are around anyway. Being able to take off our clothes helps us avoid the almost unbearable pain that comes from clothes rubbing against our skin while being sprayed with salt water.

So here we are, five naked girls in the middle of the ocean. If we meet a ship, the sailors will think that Christmas has come early.

Maybe the fact that we've stripped off is a sign of being more comfortable with each other. We see more of each other than our doctors have back home, but when there are sore backsides to check and no big mirrors, we have to rely on each other.

This all helps us get through the days. Mornings are always good. The moment the sun rises it delivers a tangible sense of relief. Someone uses the marker pen to tally another day on the side of the boat, and we exhale some of the tension that has built up through the night. The hours of darkness are difficult. The changeovers are dangerous, and there's the ever-present fear of the big waves that might lie beyond the reach of our head flashlights and the feeble navigation light.

The first daylight watch when I'm in the cabin, appreciating the stillness, I change, wash myself with baby wipes, and tidy the cabin. Because the space is so small, I have to do all of this lying down or, at best, half propped up on my elbows. It's amazing how quickly we've gotten used to living in such a small space. I'll often pray—asking God to look after Mum, saying thank you that we've made it this far, and asking for great weather to speed us across.

We often snack during the day, and because much of the food is in the hatches in Katie's and my cabin, the two of us retrieve the packs. The hatches are at the far end of the boat. The cabin is so low there that to reach into the hatches, we have to lie on our bellies, force our heads as far along as we can without getting stuck beneath the low-sloping ceiling, and stretch an arm along and down into the two-foot-deep hatch. The combination of heat, lack of fresh air, and motion of the boat as it rises and falls with the waves makes this task one of the most horrible of the crossing. Both Katie and I try to put off doing it until absolutely necessary.

On the watches when we rest, I try to sleep. At first I could sleep as much as I liked, but lately, with the weather improving, it's increasingly difficult to breathe in the cabin. But there's nowhere else to go, so I have to put up with it. When the sun is high in the sky, I lie there, sweating and fighting to suck enough oxygen from the sticky air. It's tempting to open the hatch door, but we agree that we absolutely cannot do this. If a wave landed on us while the hatch was open (which happened to one poor crew, now out of the race), everything inside the cabin would be ruined, including all the electrical equipment at the other end of the boat. The game would be over.

Having failed to brush my teeth during the first five days, I decide that I need to stick to a routine each day, and as the row progresses we work out special ways of doing things. In addition to brushing my teeth, I write in my journal, read my Bible, and listen to music.

As the day passes we chat and laugh. Every few days someone shouts from the other cabin that someone has received a message from home. We listen carefully as it is read, sharing in the happiness that each word brings. It doesn't matter that we barely knew each other before we set off; we're close now.

By our estimates we eat more than five thousand calories a day, but we burn more than that—closer to eight thousand. Having lost so much of our chocolate, we're unable to make up the difference, which explains the sound of incredible rejoicing—and even a few tears of relief—when Kate finds two jumbo-sized jars of peanut butter that we forgot about. I've always loved peanut butter, but out here my taste buds reject it.

The easygoing happiness of the day slips away with the sun. As night approaches, a sense of tension climbs aboard the boat, and each of us prepares for what is to come. The fourteen hours of darkness are always fearful times, and the threat of large waves lying in wait out of sight, ready to pounce, troubles us. We do our best to sing ourselves to happiness or talk our way to distraction, but we cannot escape the fear of the darkness.

We share our life stories—and not just the thirty-minute versions. We can tell a lot of stories in a two-hour rowing shift, and with twelve of them in a day, we share pretty intimate details. We tell each other the good, the bad, and the unrepeatable.

Not all discussions or diversions are intense. As we approach Christmas the sky gets even clearer and we play epic games of I Spy, hold mass sing-alongs to songwriters like Ed Sheeran and classics from Mariah Carey. Sometimes I listen to the sound of Helen laughing outrageously as she listens to what the comedian Ricky Gervais says through her headphones. We spend almost a whole hour playing the game of when I get to Barbados I've got to take an apple. When I get to Barbados I've got to take an apple and a banana. When I get to Barbados I've got to take an apple, a banana, and some curry . . . The monotony never becomes boring.

I discover some things that I never thought about before. One is that music is an amazingly powerful influence. Usually when somebody has a tough time, someone else starts singing a super-happy song. The words don't matter, and singing in tune makes no difference. I suspect that the worse we sing, the better the buzz we get. Within five minutes of belting out Gloria Gaynor's "I Will Survive," the boat is full of smiles and the fear slips away.

Touch really matters. It's odd to go through such a demanding physical and mental challenge in such a small space without being able to have someone give me a hug. The moments when someone places a hand on my shoulder or a leg brushes past my face during changeover are powerful. Human touch reminds me that I'm part of a community and that we are here for each other.

After the watermaker breaks, only two people row at a time. It makes us slower, but the pairs start to compete. The desire to win is common to all of us, although some are more competitive than others. I'm not sure that I'm so competitive, yet I take pride in reminding myself—and the others—that Kate and I currently hold the record for rowing the greatest distance in one watch. We manage eight miles, and the average is closer to five. The others hold the speed record: getting *The Guardian* up to 12.2 knots, or 14 miles per hour. They do it by tapping the oars at the top of a wave and then hurtling down the other side. Kate and I give it our all, but our speed record is an unimpressive 9.9 knots, or 11 miles per hour.

The competition is harmless, though, and all of us feel stripped of the need to be cool or funny or interesting. We are just being ourselves. Sometimes I think I've never been happier. Then I remember the tension among us. Most of the time it's barely noticeable. But the crescendos of stress cannot be ignored. We argue only a few times, but the main problems arise because of the perception that I have too much contact with home, and I believe that Debs, Kate, and Helen—in the aft cabin—do not work quite as hard physically as Katie and I at the other end. One of them is often pumping water, which means valuable extra time off the oars, while Katie and I are unable to miss a single shift. At night it's too dark and too dangerous for one of us to clamber across the boat to sit in the water pumping seat next to their cabin. Someone has to pump the water, and I know it's silly to make comparisons. Nevertheless, I can't seem to stop myself.

We heard about the tension among other crews becoming so intense that they stopped talking to each other entirely and did not speak to each other after reaching land. We don't want to end up like that. We learn how to address the problems. One of us blows up, and we give the person time to calm down and then to talk. If we don't talk, nothing seems to go right.

An outlet for my frustrations is writing notes for Katie in the back of my diary while I rest in the cabin. When we swap over the oars, she writes back to me. Maybe it's a bit divisive, but it helps me to know that someone here understands what I feel.

I guess that's all any of us want, isn't it? We want to be loved, to be known, and to be understood. I think about Mum, about how deeply she loves and knows and understands me, and even though I cry at the distance between us, just thinking about her love for me is enough. It's like taking in fresh oxygen. I feel stronger when I think of her, even though my cheeks are lined with tears.

My faith helps as well. This voyage—this battle with fear and fatigue and the threat of failure—has not diminished my belief in God. In fact, it is flourishing. Even though I rely on my strength and the other girls' power to get us across, I could do none of it without God. I believe without a doubt that God is at the helm.

CHAPTER 21

Golden

Invisible hands have been busy painting, but instead of carefully tracing every line, the hands have been lavish with the paint. Gold seems to be absolutely everywhere—touching every corner of the sky and across the ocean, dripping from the oars, and soaking the boat. The range of color is astounding, with light yellow at one end all the way to brazen, vibrant crimson at the other. In places the color itself is almost on fire. No palette or painting could come close. As Kate and I row, sharing this magical moment, we stare in awe as the source of this incredible light hauls itself over the horizon and into the sky. We have seen other beautiful sunrises on this crossing, but this one is different. This sunrise is fierce in its beauty, untamable.

It reminds me of the time toward the start of the row when we noticed that the water glowed at night. As our oars stroked the water, trails of brightly colored green light snaked back. I tried to lean over and cup it in my hands without luck. Katie explained that the phosphorescence was caused by tiny plankton that emit the light when the water is disturbed. But it still seems magical to me.

Before we started, I thought that each day would begin with

an outrageously beautiful sunrise and end with a bloodred sun falling back into the ocean. During the first weeks, however, the skies are gray and heavy. As we head west and a little farther south, things start to change. Sunsets are more dramatic, and though the sky seldom turns red, sometimes we sit beneath a canopy of pink and blue or one of yellow, cream, and blue. For the person pumping water in the third seat, looking past the rowers and into the west, these views are special treats.

Once the sun goes down in a cloudless sky, we sit beneath the most amazing array of stars. It's as if they form right under the water on our left and arc all the way up and over beneath the water on our right. We can see stars of all sizes—from ones that look like they're blazing just a few light-years away, to others feebly dying out billions of miles away. We see all the usual constellations, masses of shooting stars, and part of the Milky Way. Kate points out Orion's Belt and other constellations. I've slept under this sky every night of my life but never before seen it this clearly. I wonder what else I've been missing.

Sitting beneath all this distant, vast beauty, I feel small but profoundly loved and cared for. I've always thought that choosing not to believe in God is difficult, especially after staring up at a clear night sky blazoned with stars and considering the size and scale of the universe. How can we be random accidents? How can there not be something—or someone—powerful and loving behind it?

We see dolphins leap out of the water one day. They weave around the boat and look like they're dancing for us. I take photos, but they can't capture the euphoria of the moment. Here we are, in the middle of the ocean, battling our way across, and the dolphins want to play.

The bright blue vivid fish entrance us, and the birds make us feel just as reassured as the stars. Each day someone sees a bird of some kind. More than a thousand miles from land, they fly overhead. Some of them are tiny, yet they keep flying. We'd let them rest on *The Guardian* if they wanted, and we'd share some of our food with them, too, but they do not stop. We give them a little cheer and carry on our journey.

Not all nature makes us sigh and smile, though. The flying fish launch themselves onto the deck without warning, and we have to throw them back as quickly as possible. Safely pulling in a heavy oar and reaching down to grab the writhing, flapping fish are easier said than done. They freak us out a little, especially when they fly directly toward our heads. We might be five girls taking on an epic male-dominated adventure, but when those crazy flying fish start landing on us, we shriek like six-year-olds.

There are other signs that we're settling into the row. Our charts and maps are big and hard to manage so we learn how to read the moon and work out the time zone. It waxes and wanes, shifting from crescent shape to its beautifully full circle.

We learn the rhythm of the waves. The sound they produce and the motion they share with our boat are intricately linked. We can't predict what's coming, but gradually we feel less vulnerable. The waves and the wind make it possible. It's as if we've come through the trials of the early days and are now being given a reward. I like the way that sounds, but we're not even halfway through the row.

"The simple life is the best life," Mum said many times. I always nodded, but I thought that the simple life wasn't the only version of the best life on offer. I thought that you could get the best in many ways: by having fun, by being connected to people, by dreaming big and seeing those dreams come true. I thought that if you had money, you could do all the things that make you happy.

Now I'm not so sure that the simple life is just one of many good options. Out here I have everything I need, and it fits in tiny spaces. I have all the food I need, we make our water, and my cabin is dry enough to sleep in. The seawater, despite being a little painful on a cut or sore skin, leaves the rest of me feeling clean. Life is not necessarily simple—our days are still made up of twelve two-hour battles where we try to haul this boat across the ocean—but in the struggles nothing much else matters. I like it.

Many times as we row, Kate says to me, "Go on, Julia, you have thirty minutes to preach me a sermon all about love, forgiveness, hope, success, or happiness." I pick one, and off I go. I tell her stories from my life and stories from the Bible. I quote what I can and paraphrase the bits I'm not so good at remembering. But I preach it all with 100 percent conviction. Every truth I utter feels as though it comes from a deep sense of belief and understanding.

Rowing this ocean reveals someone I didn't know existed. The power of perseverance and the sense of privilege come from being one of a handful of people who see the sky and the ocean from where we are. I have been given the power to make great choices, and they have led me to this boat. I count myself blessed beyond measure.

CHAPTER 22

Not Quite Christmas Day

The excitement is high as we near Christmas. Nobody tries to pretend that it's just another day. On December 25 each person gets ten minutes on the satellite phone with the cabin door shut as she talks to loved ones back home for the first time since we left nearly three weeks ago. Christmas Day also offers a great chance to do media interviews and update supporters and sponsors.

By my calculations it's day eighteen, which makes it Christmas Eve, and I'm so excited that I ask Debs to send a message to my sister: "Tell her to remember to let all the families know about my phone interview with Sky Sports News." Debs sends the message. A few minutes later she comes out of the cabin, laughing as she reads Joy's reply: "It's Christmas Eve *tomorrow*, not today!"

As the day moves on and we move another twenty or thirty miles closer to our goal, I feel myself sinking from my upbeat mood. I think about the pressure to finish this row in time to break the world record.

Mum is also on my mind, as she has been since I began the row. I used to say that I couldn't wait to get on the boat to have a rest and leave behind all the stresses and strains that have weighed down my family over the last year or two. I might not be spending hours in hospital corridors or experiencing the panic that hits the minute my phone tells me that there's a call from my mum or sister or a blocked number, but I have not left it behind. Sometimes, when I'm alone in the cabin, the tears come with such force and speed that I dive onto my makeshift bed and bury my face in whatever clothes I can grab, hoping that they will minimize the volume of my sobbing. I feel heavy at times, and I realize that grief has me in its grasp. Mum is alive and doing better. Yet I grieve for the loss of her good health, for the troubles of home that can no longer be ignored, and for the ways that our roles have shifted. Like my sister, I have become a parent to the woman who gave us life.

This builds up within me, making my heart race and my head feel light and dizzy. Christmas Eve arrives, and I know that if I still feel this way when I speak to everyone at home tomorrow, I'll lose it. So I tell the girls that I need to talk to someone today, to try and do something to get past this. They're kind and don't make a fuss about my getting the extra contact with home. They must be worried about me.

I phone my friend Deborah. We've been close for years, and she knows me as well as anyone. She answers and is surprised to hear me, but her squeals of delight are soon drowned out by my tears. I sob on the phone for minute after minute.

"It's just so hard, Deborah. We've had all these stupid equipment failures, there have been some real tensions between us girls, and sometimes I can't breathe for the fear caused by the wind and the waves. My fingers, arms, back, legs, and skin are all in agony. I'm fed up with all this saltwater that stings all over. And I'm really, really worried that if I talk to Mum tomorrow when I'm feeling like this, it will totally freak her out. It's so hard, Deborah. It's just so hard."

Deborah's great. She just listens, then prays quickly. I feel better by the time I end the call, and by the next day, when our surprise gifts from Helen and Debs of corroded soda cans and soggy chocolate from the flooded hatch are handed around, I feel better. We wear our Santa hats, sing carols, and take turns in the cabin on the phone. We all emerge red-faced and puffy-eyed.

It's so good to talk to Mum, though she sounds frail. When I ask about what she has been doing and how she's feeling, she brushes me off. She says, "It doesn't matter. I want to hear about you." It's typical of her. I tell her a bit about the row. We end up talking about mundane things like the vegetables they're having with their turkey, and I love it. Hearing the voices of my niece, sister, and the others in the background makes me smile.

Joy makes sure that the phone is passed around so I can speak to everyone else there. She has become a mother not just to our Mum but to the whole family. I feel guilty leaving her with such a burden, and I know that she works hard to raise publicity about the row. She's amazing, but she's not immortal. I can hear the strain in her voice. She sounds tired.

Before my ten minutes are up I speak to Dad. We trade pleasantries for a few seconds. Then I say the same words that I used just after I moved back home. "I'm sorry that I have shut you out, Dad. I'm really sorry." Shutting him out has been a hard habit to break.

———

Christmas Day leaves its mark upon our rowing. We make little progress, what with the talking and the crying. But we have made it to a psychological marker. From here on, Barbados seems to urge us to row harder so we can reach it faster.

Some of the old troubles have not disappeared. Perhaps speaking to people at home stirred us up and made us feel more vulnerable. I find it hard to get over some frustrations I've been feeling for a while. I struggle with Helen and the issue of time-keeping. According to her, our changeovers should be slicker; we need to imagine that we're on a military exercise, and we cannot be late. We all agree. But when she is five minutes late taking over from me on last night's shift, I am annoyed. Five minutes may not sound like much, but they are hard to swallow when the first mate calls for excellence but does not give it.

I blow off a little steam to Katie by writing her notes in the back of my diary. I ask whether she thinks I'm wrong to feel this way. She's kind and writes nice replies. Her support means more than I can say, and I decide to talk to Debs about the changeover problems. Honestly, I think it would be easier to hold on to this frustration, but no life is to be found down that path. If I do, I'll be the loser. But if we talk, maybe things can improve.

Debs and I talk with Helen. She listens and acknowledges that the area needs addressing. People can be kind and gracious when we are honest with them. Too much of the time we aim to score points, keep our guard up, and take people down. It's a rubbish way to live, and I don't want to be a part of that anymore. I want to be honest, to like more than just the people who are like me and who *like* me. I want to be able to see the God-given good in others, learn from them, and be a nicer person to be around.

I want all these things—but not always. Sometimes I want to feel annoyed and hurt and cross.

CHAPTER 23

New Year, Old Problems

Not for the first time on this row it is dark, and I share the water with the spirits of millions of slaves. My head is filled with images of bodies piled up against each other—barely alive. These slaves who have been picked, sold, and packed up sail the waters from Africa. They head for the New World, but their story is old already. They are weak, powerless, and unable to defend themselves against those who would exploit them for profit.

I listen to an audiobook that describes the life of William Wilberforce. It takes ten hours, and I spread it over several nights. It is the story of how this British politician led the movement to abolish the slave trade. I listen to the description of his failings and his setbacks; he gave up many times, yet decided to push on for the cause in which he believed.

As I listen, I imagine what it must have been like for a woman on board a slave ship. Seasick, malnourished, forced to sleep in her excrement, crammed in with ten other people in a space barely big enough for two, prostituted and forced to serve at the stained pleasure of whatever crew was allowed to rape her.

A New World plagued by ancient problems. People inspired to

make a difference but overwhelmed by opposition. Slaves bought and sold for the pleasure and profit of others. Not much has changed in the two centuries since the days of the slave trade.

Usually I'm Miss Chatterbox, but lately I row quietly, sometimes listening to my music or my stories, sometimes sitting with the headphones in but nothing playing. These little white earbuds shield me from unwanted interaction with others. And I need that. After twenty-five days out here on the ocean, I need to allow myself to miss my family, to experience the awkward feelings inside.

In addition to missing Mum, I miss my sister. I feel a weight of guilt for leaving her at home, dealing with everything that needs dealing with right now as well as caring for a toddler and looking after Mum. She's always been gracious and supportive of this row. But it's costing her. News filters through, and we appreciate that Joy is a huge PR machine. Media coverage is so important to the cause. Hearing that she arranges to get us into another major magazine spurs us on. Our paid PR team members are also in touch, lining us up with as much as possible. A shriek of delight erupts whenever they text about setting up new interviews. There are heaps of requests for Kate; the whole of Ireland—north and south of the border—cheers her on. She's a bit freaked out by the amount of interest, but she happily obliges.

These days I feel raw and vulnerable and quiet. Most of the time I get what I need by retreating, but sometimes I need extra help. I've always believed that prayer works, and I know that there's no way that this row would have ever been possible without it.

When Deborah sends a message suggesting that I put in a call to my church on New Year's Day, I'm keen. It seems like a great idea to update everyone there on the row, build a bigger audience, and remind a few thousand people to keep praying. But Debs objects since we all couldn't call for extra comfort or support.

That's when I lose it. You can take the girl out of the ghetto, but you can't take the ghetto out of the girl! For a few minutes I'm back in Slough, flinging insults at the other end of the boat like I used to do when I was having to defend myself on the playground. Back then, attack was the only form of defense, and I tossed my insults big and fast.

I say some things to Debs that I regret and some things that I don't. "I'm proud of my church," I say, and I don't regret that. "And I'm proud that the people there have been a huge source of support for the whole row." I definitely don't regret that. "And I wouldn't have rowed the [and here's where I used a bad word, which definitely I do regret] Atlantic if not for their support. And right now I wish I had never allowed you to be skipper in the first place." I regret that last statement most of all.

Nobody rows during this back-and-forth.

"Well," says Debs, "I'm fine if you want to take over and be skipper for the rest of the journey." I wince inside. The argument quickly loses oxygen, and I go back into my cabin. It seems too small for my anger and hurt. The thought of being skipper for the rest of the row is laughable, mainly because I don't have a clue what I'm doing out here. Debs has been doing all the navigating and doing it well. She has taken on extra watches when others have been too sick to row. Debs has always filled in the gaps—and without complaining. Whatever needs doing, she does, losing precious sleep in the process.

So why am I mad at her? I guess I'm frustrated that I never learned how to operate a lot of the equipment, and I have to depend on the others. I don't like feeling dependent; I don't like feeling weak; I don't like feeling scared. But I am all three. I'm wounded and vulnerable, and I need time to breathe and calm down.

Eventually it's time for me to row again, and with Kate rowing between us, Debs and I talk. "I'm so sorry, Debs. And I want to apologize to all of you," I say to the rest of the girls.

The whole adventure started out as my baby, but I have to acknowledge that is no longer the case. It belongs to all of us, yes, but Debs and Helen can do things that I can't. I have been holding on too tightly. I have to let go.

Later on, as I feel the sun slipping out of the sky behind my back, I put on the headphones once more. But I'm not doing it to escape or to hide. I need to listen again to the story of how the slave trade was beaten. I need to be reminded that these people used their influence the best they could, and when it wasn't enough they tried again. I need to be reminded of the importance of not giving up. I need to be reminded that good things come from sacrifices made repeatedly.

Kate and I are alone with the oars in our hands. The sea plays up again, sending me two different heights of waves. My hands and eyes and arms must work extra hard to make sure that each oar makes a good connection with the water. I pull forward on my legs, sliding my seat toward my heels. I push my arms forward, glance at the water, and drop the oars in, pushing back on my legs as I pull both wrists toward me. How much closer have I sent us to Barbados? A few inches? A few feet? Katie has worked out that each of us will need to make 657,260 strokes to get us across.

It's a colossal number to get my head around. But I can break it down. I just have to do this stroke, then another, then another. It's all I can do.

I can't end human trafficking any more than I can turn myself into a saint, but I can take this one stroke and inch my way closer toward these goals I'm desperate to reach. And most important, I can't do it on my own.

CHAPTER 24

Change

I find my phone this morning. It is still wrapped in its plastic bag, shoved into a hat, and buried beneath some clothes at the bottom of my kit bag. I used it on that first day, sending silent messages to my sister as we edged away from La Gomera, but I haven't touched it since. When the signal dropped off, I felt as though I had jumped out of a plane but had forgotten to check my parachute. Would I cope?

It turns out that I'm fine without my phone. The little rectangle of glass and lights that *never* leaves my side has been switched off for the last thirty days, and I don't miss it. I didn't see that change coming.

I can see changes happening in some of the other girls. Kate, who is ten years younger than me, started out as a quiet, introverted, gentle girl. She's been out of university just a few months—a year at most—and she's one of the youngest people taking part in the challenge. But she's grown every day. So much of the time Kate pushes us on, reminding us that we can do this row, that we have the strength. Her knee is often in agony from operating the foot steering, but she calls out the encouragement, acting as team

163

coach and chief motivator. And confidence has started to flourish within her as a result. She holds her head higher now than when we started. What will this flourishing, confident young woman do once she steps off the boat and starts thinking about real life again? I know she will thrive at anything she chooses.

Helen has changed too. She's had it hard with near-constant nausea and terrible sores, but she has also been through some tough times emotionally. Yet over the course of the row, something releases and softens within her.

Change for me has been more like Kate's gradual shift than Helen's dramatic turnaround. The sea has been working at me, smoothing my rough edges of ego and pride. It's almost as though I have been able to watch parts of myself disappear. I'd be lying if I said I hadn't felt pleased at times about the row, especially before it started. But once it began, there was no room for egos on board. Not that I've been made into a saint, but I know that I can't rely on feeling important to give me what I want.

Because of the row I want to be a better person. I want to be teachable. I want to learn. I want to grow. I still feel bad about the argument between Debs and me on New Year's Day. I reacted so poorly because I felt so misunderstood. My words came out wrong that day. I've never felt as though I could appoint anyone to be skipper. I never felt as though I had the casting vote, but I have believed in this row with every ounce of my passion. I've thrown myself into it, and I know that if I hadn't been so dedicated, it probably would not have gotten beyond the harbor. But it's hard to share something you care about so much. Yet I'm learning to hold things lightly as I try to lead with strength and kindness. It's one big balancing act, but I'm up for it.

The differences between how my life used to be and how it

is now are coming into focus. It was so polished, so (almost) perfect, but it wasn't working. Trying to appear in control was a lie. Gradually I recognize that my life was a long, long way from perfect. So getting on this boat has been a struggle between the old part of me and the new. It has been a struggle between the part of me that wants to appear strong (but is really weak) and the part that is weak (but can be truly strong).

If I'm honest, I've always felt quite average. I did not excel at anything at school, not academically at least. Sports came naturally, but study was an effort. I've gotten used to beating myself up, comparing myself to others and never feeling that I match up. But I've had to learn many new things on this row, and many of those lessons have come from being stripped of the things that I used to rely on.

Some of my friends are married. I can sense this longing in me to be married and settled down when I get home, but I don't want to add another layer of security that won't address my deepest needs. I hope I will get married and have kids one day, but I don't want to do either because I need a badge that confirms my identity. I don't want to do it so that I can say I am a wife and mother because that's what I think I should be doing at my age. I want to do it when I'm ready, not a moment before.

Another side of me knows that being single gives me opportunities. I sacrificed my friendships and social life to make this row. There was no room for romance, and even if a guy wanted to get to know me, I wouldn't have noticed him. I've accepted that, and I think I still will when I get home. These are my days to work hard, to serve, to fight for the cause, and to dedicate myself to helping Mum. When the seasons finally change, maybe I will have the opportunity to invest in someone.

So here I am, finally waking up to the fact that I need people but not in the way I think I needed them before. I cannot do life alone, especially when I face a situation as difficult as this one. Just admitting it feels freeing.

Fear has been my greatest teacher out here. I've always been scared of the dark, and as a child I could not sleep without a night light. I don't remember a night when Mum was more than a few steps away. As an adult I've been safety conscious and avoided dark alleys and parking lots. But there's no Mum to soothe me here, and when the moon hides behind the clouds and the hatch door is sealed shut, my fears are those of my childhood. Only, this time, monsters are out there—great big ones, thirty feet tall, waiting to fall on me unannounced.

I still don't like the dark, and I still close my eyes and pray that the waves won't take us down, but I don't feel it as strongly as I once did. Because it has started to get so hot in the day, the cooler nights have meant that I begin to enjoy the comfort brought by the darkness. It's funny how your fears can become your friends when you push through.

It's also more than the way I respond to danger. As I sit pumping water, listening to the slap and swoosh of the waves, and imagining the hundreds of miles behind us that we have traveled, I'm struck by the thought that if I can do this, I can attempt almost anything. We all can.

Is it too early to be thinking like this? I don't see it that way. Even if we fail to break the record or finish this row, we've come so far and overcome so much self-doubt and difficulty that this voyage has been a success. It has taught me that I'm stronger, braver, and tougher than I think.

Feeling almost invincible, I decide to answer nature's call and make a trip to the bucket. I must be distracted because as I finish my business, stand up, and clean the bucket, Debs points out that I've got poo running all the way down my leg. After a little laugh from us all and a quick cleanup with the baby wipes, I pump water again. I'm different now.

CHAPTER 25

The First Person to
See Barbados

With our backs facing west to Barbados and our faces looking east in the direction of La Gomera, we always look for
the sunrise. Sometimes it's easier to spot than others. Sometimes
the cloud that hugs the horizon reveals itself quickly, taking just
a few minutes to peek out of the darkness before changing like a
chameleon from battleship gray to smoke white, then pale-colored
flesh, pink, and golden red. Other times, when the sky is clear,
it's as if the sun has to battle against the whole of space in order
to be seen. On those days the sun spreads out, and one by one the
stars retreat. Nighttime shrinks away, and we get out the marker
pen and slice another black line onto the tally on the boat. One
day closer.

Whatever the start, every day brings the same calculations and
questions about the one thing that seems most important right
now—the world records. "Are we on? Are we on?" Katie, our math
whiz, helps us keep track of our progress and potential. And every
day the same answer comes back: "Yes, we're still on!"

As long as the weather doesn't drastically deteriorate or a vital piece of equipment doesn't break, we should be fine. Yet the nearer we get, the harder Kate and I pray. Even believing that God was on our side throughout, I won't take it for granted that we've made it until our feet are firmly on dry land. My constant prayer is this: *Please, Lord, let us get there.* After all, who wants to hear about five girls who nearly made it to Barbados?

Considering that we're about six hundred miles from the end and get constant reassurances that the weather is holding out, we generally feel good about our chances of not getting blown drastically off course. As for the boat, that's a different story, and it all depends on how you choose to tell it. The pessimist would point to the long list of equipment failures—the battery tester, the Autohelm, the watermaker, the foot steering, and the holes in the hull—and say that our chances of making it through the next two or more weeks without more breakdowns are slim. At least three of us on this boat are confirmed optimists, and we believe that everything that *can* break has *already* broken. What else can go wrong?

Regular updates on our overall standing in the race encourage us. We started at the back, of course, but we moved up from eighteenth to a pretty decent fifth. We are more determined to push hard to the finish. Besides, we're in a cat-and-mouse fight with the two firefighters from Wales, *Atlantic Dash*, who currently hold the fourth position. The race organizers sense that there's a bit of healthy competition between us, and they do what they can to stir things up a bit. It's all good fun and probably helps us push harder.

So we're on it. We know the pace of our row, the route to take, and the need to be slick with our changeovers. The record stands at fifty days, and by our calculations we stand to beat it, hopefully by a couple of days.

All of this is background to what comes next. First, we get a message from Alex at the PR company. We have received lots of messages from Alex and his colleagues, some of them about forthcoming interviews, others about press coverage of us, and even one about what a certain footballer and his wife named their baby. The world of the London-based PR firm seems a long, long way from ours.

This message from Alex is simple: "We need to speak to you urgently." We're mystified. What could it be about? Has he landed unimaginably good coverage? Has something gone wrong? "What's wrong?" we reply.

Because we turn on our sat phone only an hour a day, by the time his message has come through nobody is in his office. We have to wait another few hours before we can get ahold of anyone there. The tension and speculation grow until we receive a reply.

It reads: "You're not going to get the record."

The atmosphere on the boat crashes with more force and speed than a fifty-foot wave. We've worked so hard, come so far, and rowed so fast. We're convinced we're on target to be the fastest female crew across the Atlantic. What does Alex know that we don't? Did we get the record wrong? Have we miscounted the number of days we've been out here?

We can't work it out. Katie and Debs are sure about the numbers, and we're all sure about the record as it stands. How can we have suddenly slipped so far off the pace? We're a bit cross but mainly devastated. We've failed before we've even finished. It feels worse than being capsized or being struck by a submerged container. Worst of all, we've lost hope of gaining the media spotlight and the chance to shout our hearts out about the nightmare of modern-day slavery.

The phone spits out another message. A few hours have passed since the message from Alex that left us winded, and Debs says that this new one is from him too. Perhaps he feels that he's given us some space and now can give us the rest of the info. We listen in silence as Debs reads it: "Sorry, girls. I forgot that you left two days after the whole fleet. You're still on course for the record after all! Much love, Alex."

The shock gives way to relief and then anger. As one we thicken the air with our words.

"What the heck's wrong with them?"

"Do they not realize how hard this is out here?"

"Do they not understand how much it means to us to arrive in Barbados as record holders?"

"Do they not know that we are literally working our butts off out here?"

We hit other rough patches at this time, but none quite like this one. The boat holds up for us, and nothing else breaks down. The weather behaves, and on day thirty-eight we notice a strange yellow tinge to the ocean. It takes awhile for the change to register. Kate and I are so used to staring at the same old deep gray and blue of the ocean. Looking closer we see that wheat-colored stuff, which looks a little like hay, floats around us. Kate realizes that it's seaweed. The water is getting warmer, which means we must be closer to Barbados than we imagined.

So many people told us that we should try hard to enjoy the last week or two because the days will pass quickly. The trouble is, we get a little ahead of ourselves with excitement about getting close to the end of the row. We talk so much about what we're going to eat when we land that we dream about it. One night I'm pumping water when Kate emerges from the cabin. Half-asleep, she waves her empty hand in front of her and tells Debs to come and have a taste of the chicken burger she just bought.

When I'm awake and I can spare the concentration, I let my mind drift to thoughts of freshly squeezed orange juice and a plate of fresh fruit. I crave both, which is odd because I haven't been too unhappy about the expedition food. But almost anything to do with life on land has an almost magical appeal now. Throughout the row Kate and I have been talking about the things we want to do at home: standing up, walking and talking with friends, and driving. Sleeping on clean, dry, fresh linen is too much to bear! Having a meal with friends? Paradise.

The row has fallen into three phases. First, there was the initial shock of it. Everything went wrong, the seasickness was debilitating, and the combination of fear and grief left me absolutely shell-shocked. Second, the elements became less difficult, and we just got our heads down and rowed hard. I wonder whether we all retreated a little into ourselves at that point—I know I did—and from these private, well-defended places came the hurt and insecurity that resulted in our conflicts. I think we had only three proper arguments during the whole crossing, which is fewer than people warned us we'd have. Third, with a few hundred miles left to go, we've relaxed into it. It'll be over soon enough, and I already miss it.

Until this point in the row our contact with home has been limited, but with the end apparently in sight, we decide to talk more often with the people we care about. Doing that is bittersweet for me because the focus of my conversations with Mum and Joy is whether Mum will be well enough to make the flight to Barbados to be there when we land. I want to see and hug her more than anything in the world, and knowing that she could be standing there, her face beaming as we arrive, is a thought so sweet and life-giving that it makes me smile and almost giggle out loud. But Mum doesn't sound strong, and my conversations with Joy make it clear that flying Mum so far is too risky. Nevertheless, for a few days the verdict swings between yes and no, and I ride the waves of happiness as I consider the possibilities. The inevitable happens, and Joy tells me that Mum just isn't strong enough to make the trip. I know that is the right call, but that doesn't make it any easier to accept. I cry a long time. I miss Mum; it's as simple as that. The girls, of course, are brilliant as they try to comfort me.

Before I sink too low, I remember about trying to be patient and recognizing that while we can't change our circumstances, we can choose how we react to them. I remind myself of how good the rain feels; it is bliss to untie my hair and comb the rain through it with my fingers. We do not wash our hair at any point during the crossing, even though we have small bottles of shampoo that we planned to use on Christmas Day. Having to pump extra water makes the notion too overwhelming. As the warm, fresh rainwater pours over us, we try to scrape off some of the salt and sunscreen caked on our skin, although I can't really do battle with the dreadlocks that are forming in my hair. It feels good to give in to this simple pleasure but it also feels good to have to wait.

We've been in touch with a few of the other crews, and the *Atlantic 4* told us that when they were about one hundred miles out they saw the glow in the night sky above Barbados—slightly less than two days of good rowing away. We were three hundred miles behind them then, and over the next two days we imagined them pulling into the harbor, making it onto dry land, celebrating with their loved ones, eating chicken burgers, drinking orange juice, and sleeping all night long on a bed that didn't move or squeak with damp.

We are inspired, knowing that within five days or so we may see Barbados. So we press on, but the days drag, and the horizon seems to reveal just more horizon. As the air temperature rises and the sun shines, the cabins become unbearably hot.

Good news comes on the sat phone. We've pulled ahead of *Atlantic Dash*, and we're now in fourth. Our friends in the *Atlantic 4* have already made it into Port St. Charles, Barbados, finishing in third place behind two very fast crews—one that has set a new world record for the fastest solo crossing of the Atlantic. It took the guy forty days to get across, while the *Atlantic 4* did it in forty-one. Katie tells us that we should get in at forty-five days; we'll comfortably be the fastest all-female crew and the first crew of five women. Kate is set to be the first Irish woman to row an ocean, and I am the first Finnish person, so the excitement is high. But we don't want to slow down or put anything at risk, so we dig deep and row with all our strength. Each watch takes everything we've got, and I crawl back into the stuffy cabin exhausted, picturing the largest glass of orange juice I've ever seen.

I think I'm dreaming when I hear someone talking about seeing land, but I soon wake up enough to get my head out of the half-lit cabin and look to where the others are pointing. There, hiding in the distance against the early-morning sky—so faint it's possible to miss it—is the orange glow of man-made light. I never knew that light pollution could look so incredibly beautiful and exciting.

Of course, we have another problem. The runners on the middle seat squeak terribly as metal tears against metal. We rub antibacterial hand gel on it as lubrication, but it's only a matter of time before the gel runs out or the seat fails altogether. The third seat is already broken and is being used as the water-pumping station, so the potential loss of this middle seat is serious. If it goes only one person will be able to row at any one time. And ahead of us is the final battle: wicked currents as well as a huge coral reef that will take us out if we drift too close.

I sleep again. But this time I do not dream of juice. I dream of capsizing.

CHAPTER 26

The Final Day

11:00 A.M.

Today was supposed to be so very different than it is. I had it
worked out in my mind as I planned every detail. Even before we
squeezed ourselves aboard this crazy little boat forty-five days ago,
I'd created a script for the day we reached the other side. And God
knows how my mind has turned to this day during the row. When
the waves and fear have reared up in equal measure, like childhood
nightmares, I've found comfort in the idea of starting my final
shift, eating my final meal, and taking my final strokes.

I'd always assumed that by now I'd be exhausted but satisfied, desperate to get off the boat and onto land, feeling as though
a great adventure was over. Those feelings don't fit this moment,
however.

I'd just finished my second turn at the oars and entered the
cabin when Debs spotted Barbados. As she called out to us, she
called an end to our beautiful, painful journey. I'm not sure that
I'm ready for it to end.

In the cabin it's as if nothing changed. I can feel the familiar rhythm as the boat rises and falls, tilts and leans with the waves. I can hear the familiar sounds—the gentle whack as the oars hit the water, the slap as the top of a wave breaks free and launches itself at the hull. Whatever we're feeling, I guess we're all feeling it deeply. No one talks much.

I look out and check on Barbados. It's slowly growing bigger as the sun climbs through the sky. Seeing land after so much water seems strange. All my life I've believed I could trust land. Water was dangerous; water could kill. But I don't see things quite the same way now. Here I have all that I need—food, shelter, water, and friends. On land life will be complicated.

I'm going to miss this boat, and I'm going to miss these people. I'm going to miss eating candy every two hours and seeing the way the sun paints life across my whole body as it rises in the morning sky. I'm going to miss night skies, so full of stars that I think I am on another planet, and the way it feels to know that in this very moment, I am in the middle of one of my life's greatest adventures. I'm going to miss the feeling that I have all I need in the here and now. I hope I can hold on to some changes that these weeks have started to grow in me.

But I also have goose bumps as I think about what's coming next: holding my sister, hearing my mother's voice tell me about what she's having for her evening meal or what she sees as she looks out of her window, and experiencing the chaos and craziness of the media blitz.

8:00 P.M.

Red and green lights hover just above the water, approaching us at speed. The tension's getting to me, and it takes awhile to realize that this is not an alien abduction but good old Simon and Gemma on a small yacht leading *Aurora* out to meet us a few miles away from the port.

Soon after they reach us, I recognize a voice among the screaming, whooping, and singing: "Girls! Girls! Here come the girls!" My sister could always shout loudly, but this time her voice carries across the waves and through the darkness.

Gemma and Simon radioed us a couple of hours ago that the bravest of our family and friends were going to climb aboard the support boat, *Aurora*, and come out and cheer us on for the final couple of hours. Now we can just about see the deck lights off our port bow, but my sister's voice announces their arrival, calling to us from I don't know how far away.

We're already wearing the special T-shirts that are covered with the sponsors' names. We'd have to do it all over if we forgot to put them on for the arrival. And then *Aurora* slips into view for a few seconds as it circles us like a shark. The darkness feels heavier and thicker than ever, hiding her from us, but since we're so near the end we figure that we don't have to worry about the broken battery tester anymore. We turn on all our deck lights, and we are soaked in light. For the first time in the row we can see ourselves at night, and the darkness beyond slips far away. Having so much illumination feels like one of the greatest luxuries of my life.

Now we can see *Aurora* when she tacks and passes us for a second time. To say that she is breathtaking is a cliché, but in this case it's entirely true. She didn't seem that big when we saw her in the marina in La Gomera, but next to our little boat she looks like a mountain. But there's not much time to think about that because within minutes she shines a crazily bright light on us. It almost blinds us, but eventually Aurora is alongside. I can hear our wonderful friends and loved ones but not see them yet, so I imagine them hanging over the side, hugging and waving and screaming and smiling and taking photos. So near but so far.

The sensation I've been feeling since Debs announced that she'd seen land, the one that turned my insides upside down and sent shivers up and down my back, well, someone just turned the power way up. I feel alive like never before. I desperately want to wave but dare not stop rowing because we have to pull so hard. I settle for shouting back to Joy, and as I fill my lungs and prepare to yell we take a hit from a big wave off the starboard bow. It sends me flying out of my seat with the oars scraping my knees. They're already covered in scars and bruises, so one or two more won't make much difference. It's a vivid reminder of everything that we were told before the start of the row: "If there's one place that you're likely to capsize, it's coming into Barbados. The currents will force you out, the waves will take you sideways, and the wind could be coming from anywhere. You have to remember to concentrate here."

As if on cue, the wind picks up, and the waves turn nasty. Suddenly, this doesn't feel like a victory lap. The next two hours that it will take us to get into the harbor will be tough. *Aurora* has been circling us like we're sheep in a field, guiding us to safety. But as much as the wind and waves trouble us, the people on *Aurora's* deck have it worse. Many of them are novices on the sea, just like we were more than 3,000 miles ago. They struggle with the pitch and roll, and every few minutes someone else holds onto the rails, leans over, and pukes violently down the side the of hull.

Eventually they radio to say they're heading back into the port, leaving us alone again. I look at Katie, Kate, Debs, and Helen, and I smile. "We're doing it, girls! We're rowing the Atlantic!"

The joke's tired now, and they hurl abuse at me, laughing all the time. That's how we've gotten here, with a lot of laughter (as well as fear and frustration). Another wave breaks over us and drenches me. Forty-five days on the water, and I can't stop myself from making a face and retching whenever I get a mouthful of seawater.

MIDNIGHT

Whatever I was thinking about this morning—all that stuff about missing this boat and feeling strange about coming back to land—I want to take it back. I'm ready to get off.

We were supposed to be on land a couple of hours ago. Simon told us that the harbormaster goes home at 10:00 p.m. on Saturday. If we were late, we'd have to spend another night on the ocean. Thankfully he changed his mind, although who knows how they persuaded him to stay on. Maybe they told him we were naked.

Helen has been in constant radio contact with Simon and Gemma in their boat. They are doing all they can to guide us in, while Debs and Kate are at the oars for the last watch. Our hoped-for two-hour journey to reach dry land has stretched almost to four hours. We battle to avoid crashing on the coral reef and get beyond the harbor walls.

After *Aurora* left us, the waves and wind conspired to keep us out and shook us about. Kate's foot took such a beating that I am on my knees, operating the foot steering with my hands to help her. I'm the only one who can see where we're going, and I call out words of encouragement to Debs and Kate, who are amped up on adrenaline. I tell them that we're nearly there. I'm lying.

With the three of us on deck it's crowded. There's no room for Helen to join us and squat over the bucket to do the wee that she's been holding for hours. She has to stay in her cabin and try to pee into one of the big and almost empty jars of peanut butter. If the waves were calmer, we'd be in hysterics about it, but laughing is not an option right now. We have to keep battling to get through.

As we left La Gomera, the acceleration zone picked us up and hurled us out, as if the ocean was welcoming us with its oversized arms. But now the ocean and its famous current don't want to let us go. I lose count of the big waves. An epic one sends us over on a 90-degree capsize. I stare at the water beside me and thank God that all our foot leashes are secure.

Although this is perhaps one of the hardest moments of all, I feel at peace. This moment with these waves will pass, and at some time tonight or tomorrow, we will stand on dry land after doing what we set out to do as a team. Humans aren't built to be alone. We're made to work with others, not be isolated and vulnerable.

For the last two years I've heard myself described by friends, colleagues, rowing coaches, sponsors, and the media as someone who "plans to row across the Atlantic." Now I'm going to be known as someone who has done it. How will it sound when I tell someone two or three years from now that I took part in this row? Will this be one of my life's shining highlights, or will it be the first in a string of bold adventures? I hope the latter is true.

The land looks so dark, and it is so quiet too. I'm surprised that it feels so alien. The idea of getting off this little boat and back onto solid earth isn't quite as reassuring as I thought it would be. Part of me is desperate to get back and hug my sister and everyone else, but another part of me wants to stay on the water forever.

Now sheltered from the wind by rowing as close to the land as possible, we can hear people cheering from a distance. Maybe *Aurora* has come back to us to help out. I can't tell, but I try to see as I steer away from the coral reef that I guess is to our port side. Then, before anyone else, I see it. "Look!" I say. "The sky! The sky!"

I look up and see a low cloud dyed a deep red, resting low on the water. I can't make out what it is, but it's beautiful.

"Flares," says Helen. "They're lighting flares."

The final moments of a battle are some of the hardest to push through. It's as if the ocean is asking us one last time, "Do you really want this? Do you really have the strength to fight your way through?" We push on toward the light, toward the land.

CHAPTER 27

The End and the Beginning

It has been an avalanche of firsts. My first steps on dry land in forty-five days. My first taste of fresh fruit. My first shoes. My first locked door. My first shower. My first bed. My first sleep that lasted more than two hours. My first chance to be awakened by someone other than Katie, Helen, or Debs. My first chance to stare out at the ocean and not have to worry about foot leashes, wind patterns, or partially submerged containers.

Arriving last night was wild. We staggered onto the jetty, helped by the *Atlantic 4* who held out their hands to us, popping the champagne corks and waving the flares high overhead. What came next is still a blur, but the feelings are clear. Overwhelming relief, a sense of safety, and a whole lot of disbelief. Had we really done it? Had we really rowed the Atlantic?

Almost everything about the world seemed different. Flip-flops felt like lead weights on my feet, and cars seemed to drive at such incredible speeds that I started to freak out a bit, even though I knew they were crawling along the roads at their usual speed. To be surrounded by so many people—friends, family, media, strangers—was odd, too, and all the colored flags and flashlights added to the tapestry. My body was exhausted, but soon my brain felt just as overwhelmed. We'd done what we set out to do: established a new Guinness World Record for the first female crew of five to row an ocean, and broken the existing record for the fastest female crew across the Atlantic. And Kate's now the first Irish woman ever to have rowed the Atlantic, and I'm the first Finn ever to have rowed an ocean.

We arrived sometime past 1:00 a.m., but I didn't get to bed until four hours later. Time stopped in those first hours on land. There was too much celebrating to be done to sleep, and by the time we'd staggered up to the customs office and had our passports stamped with the words *Entry by Row Boat*, the whole night became even more surreal.

But I slept, sandwiched between my sister and my friend Laura, on a bed made with clean white sheets. The room's balcony looks out over white sand to the ocean beyond. It looks so tranquil and so small from here.

This is where my work starts. It's 9:00 a.m. in Barbados, but the day is halfway over in England. We have a moment to talk to people about the row and share the reason behind it, but that moment won't last forever. So I get up, and I do the first of many interviews. I start with Sky Sports News, my employer and supporter and home to many friends. I can hear my words coming out, and I sound dumbstruck, not at all like someone who makes a living putting together television programs.

For six and a half weeks we lived in a bubble—at times a frustrating, terrifying, maddening, rage-inducing bubble—but it was home. I was desperate to get to Barbados, but now I have to readjust to life as it was before my big adventure. I'm not so sure that life as it was before is on the menu anymore.

———————

Having been back for less than two days, all of us start to suffer physically. We experience unbelievably painful leg cramps as the muscles tighten like they've been filled with cement. We walk as if we carry an invisible weight on our backs. Massages help, but they're agony. We're told by other crews that it's normal. It's the body's way of readjusting to a new routine that doesn't revolve around twelve hours of intense physical exercise a day.

Only after two days do I find the energy to wash my hair, and though the saltwater drains away after my first shower, I can't quite get rid of the ocean smell deep in my skin.

Our feet are in a bad way with an array of blisters, sores, and general damage, and the skin hangs off. A woman I've come to for a pedicure on the third day after our arrival looks horrified at their condition. Our feet and toenails are white and waterlogged, but the other parts of our bodies don't look too bad. We have deep tans, the weight we deliberately gained before the row is gone, and we feel toned. If only we could stand up straight.

The interviews keep coming, and I get used to answering the same questions. Everyone wants to know how long it took, how I feel, what I ate, and how I slept. I introduce the topic of the modern-day slave trade into these conversations, and to my surprise, I easily guide the conversation around to talk about why we did the row. People really do want to know about this terrible wrong.

I also talk a little about our difficulty in readjusting. In the evening when everyone heads out to eat together, I want to be on my own in my room. I'm exhausted. A polar expedition leader sends us a message that what we are going through, trying to fit back into our normal sleeping patterns, is perfectly normal, and given time, it will pass.

Eating "normal" food brings me joy like never before. The expedition foods and sweets we had subsisted on have left me craving fresh, healthy food. Pineapple and melon send my taste buds into a wild state—I'm literally drooling as I eat. I savor a meal that includes flying fish, not only because it tastes amazing but because I feel like I'm getting revenge on all the fish that hit us during the row.

Any sense of my wanting to be back on the boat vanishes the moment we go back on board and clean the thing. We take our friends and family with us, armed with plenty of rubber gloves, and we take out our forty-five days' worth of food packaging, used baby wipes, and general rubbish. We didn't dump anything into the ocean that didn't belong there, so some of this stuff has formed into disgusting mold. We're all shocked by how tiny the boat looks. How did we manage to live on it?

———

Ten days after we arrive in Barbados, it's time to fly home. The journey—the reverse of which took us forty-five days, fifteen hours, and twenty-six minutes, needed more than three million pulls on the oars, and required each of us to burn about eight thousand calories per day—is over in a flash. I step back into the wind and snow in London, deeply tanned but surrounded by my fellow Brits with their pale January skin. I'm wearing my "We Rowed the Atlantic" T-shirt and shorts, but the cold doesn't matter. I've been through worse.

I have to do two things as soon as we land. First, we head over to a TV studio and do a live interview where we are served cocktails and share some of our expedition food with the interviewer. And then, after saying good-bye to everyone but Debs and another friend who stay with me for support, I go home to see Mum.

When I see her, she reminds me of my grandmother. She is hunched over, and the weight has slipped from her already tiny body. Her legs stumble like Bambi as she tries to rush over to hug me as I walk through the door. All of a sudden Mum looks really old.

I don't want her to know that I'm upset. I hope she'll assume my tears are a sign of relief and joy at seeing her again, not terrible sadness. We hug a long time, and then we talk.

"I didn't think I'd ever see you again," she says.

I'm surprised. "Really, Mum?" What happened to that early confidence that she displayed when I first told her about the row? What about the way she seemed so strong, so much better, before I left? Had she deteriorated so much during the row, or had I not seen how bad she was before I left?

"Honestly, I would go to bed at night trying to imagine what it was like for you. And I didn't think I was going to see you again."

Again, I'm reminded of how selfless and loving this woman is. Her body is falling apart, her marriage has been a challenge for years, and yet she fully supported my heading off on an adventure that she didn't think I'd survive. I look at the weight she's lost and the years she's gained, and I feel heavy with guilt.

Mum sits down, and I look around the apartment for the first time. It's as if the rooms have been suffering in step with Mum. I'd been living here with her before the row, but while I was away Dad moved in with her. I've always been obsessively tidy. He never has, but even by his standards the place is a wreck. It is not just untidy but unclean. A large patch of the carpet is wet with urine. It must be Mum's, and I don't think Dad has cleaned it properly.

Within minutes of being at Mum's and within hours of being back in the country, the row feels so distant that I'm wondering whether I was a part of it.

As if this return to reality isn't brutal enough, the next day I have to take Mum to a hospital appointment. I'm relieved that I've not forgotten how to drive, but as we wait in the cold hospital corridor, I crumble inside. I've wanted so much for the things I've learned on the row to stay with me, and even though I knew it would be tough to come back home, I was certain that I'd have a little longer before the crash came. Surely I'd make it past the twenty-four-hour mark before the buzz wore off?

One more cruel blow is to come: seeing Dad again. Having left before I returned to see Mum, he comes to the apartment one or two days later, and I immediately feel the familiar tides of anger swell up within me. "I'm cross about the state you've let Mum live in, Isi. Really cross." I try to hold back, but it's too hard. The last time we spoke was Christmas Day, when I apologized for shutting him out. Now, I can't find that compassion. I want all the old defenses up and all the old weapons at the ready. This relationship is going to take more than an ocean row to fix. But I really do want it to be better.

The question is, can it be? I think it can. In the course of the row something within my heart changed. Even the shock and frustration that rise up within me don't last as long as they used to.

Once again I think of the cause. I think of Alejandra. I remind myself of how hard it was for her to reintegrate into normal life. I get a better perspective as a result. My situation is nothing in comparison. I don't have to be dragged down by this. With God's help, I can do better.

CHAPTER 28

The Missed Bottle

There's a part of the row that I don't think I've ever discussed. In front of every crowd, at every dinner table, at every conference filled with nice-looking people in suits, I've not told about seeing the bottle with a message in it.

It was Christmas Day. We'd cried after we'd spoken with our loved ones at home. I was rowing again, late in the afternoon, and all was quiet. Perhaps that's why I was more attentive to the water than usual. My eye was drawn to a patch of light to my right. The waves often reflected the light, but this was different—sharper and bigger. Right there, in the middle of the Atlantic Ocean, there was a light blue gin bottle. I watched in silence as it floated about six feet from the boat. We passed it, and I saw a piece of paper inside. I don't know why I didn't say anything, but I watched the bottle disappear from view.

Why didn't I say something? Why didn't I stop rowing, jump in, and grab the bottle? It would have made a great story, and who knows, maybe the message inside was important. There were so many reasons not to stop. I was too focused, too slow to react, too worried that the others might think I was dumb to chase such a childish dream, too scared of getting into the water and not being able to return to the boat.

Human trafficking is like the bottle that I never stopped to grab. It is hard to spot, yet once we finally see, hear, or read about it, there's an ocean full of reasons why we choose to ignore it. We can be too busy concentrating on our lives to want to pause. We can be too slow to react and definitely too worried about what other people will think. It asks us to risk something—our comfort, our time, and the safety of life as normal. Once we reach out for it, things might never be the same again.

In the years following our arrival in Barbados a lot has changed. Steph, who was the first one to come up with the idea of rowing the ocean, is no longer single. She and Joe—the guy who loaned us his boat to help get the people at church excited about the row—fell in love and were on their way to be married. Her decision to back out of the row led her to meet Joe, and her life changed forever. For me, the decision that mattered was saying yes to the row, even though I felt I had nothing to give. We made opposite decisions, but both led to brilliant outcomes. Sometimes we have to be prepared to surrender things that we think are most precious to us.

And Mum? The row was hard for her; she was vulnerable the whole time I was away. That was a dangerous place for her, but she's much better now. Immobility and muscle spasms trouble her, but I can honestly say the twinkle is back in her eyes. She's been diagnosed with Parkinson's, and even though that news is worrisome, the doctors can start treating her effectively. She is no longer on the medication to ease her depression, and she is beginning to feel that her body is hers again. She's getting stronger, and I feel optimistic about her. Mum is back.

What about Dad? I love him. When he and I are together alone, we're at our best and able to build up our relationship. When Mum is around, though, I want to be her protector. I am still guilty of pushing him away. They say that forgiving someone is a continual process. I want to be able to offer that to Dad, but I have a long way to go. Deep down, I think I can do it because the greatest gift from my parents was my faith. Although Dad didn't provide the material trappings, he gave me the greatest, priceless gift. How can I not be optimistic about change?

Since completing the row I have digested and reflected on the row and the events preceding it. I've thought about the things I've learned and the ways I've changed. On the ocean I'd often repeat bits of the Bible to myself out loud. I'd remind myself that "I can do all things through Christ who strengthens me," "When you pass through the waters, I [God] will be with you," and we should "not become weary in doing good, for at the proper time we will reap a harvest if we do not give up."[1] They helped then, and they help now.

I've thought a lot about fear. Some people think that once you've rowed across an ocean you no longer fear anything. They believe that by taking on the waters and winning, you reach dry land having changed into something altogether different. It's a nice idea, and I think that before the row a part of me hoped it would be true as well. I really liked the idea of becoming a new version of myself without a sense of fear. But it's not true.

I still know what fear tastes like, but something has changed within me. I suppose it has a little to do with getting to know what fear looks like when you get up really close. Most of the time fear has us diving for cover, turning to whatever distractions we prefer in order to help us forget what it is like to feel scared. But ever since those phone calls from my father and sister telling me that Mum was in terrible trouble, I've not been able to hide. And once we were out on the ocean, there was no escaping the darkness or the impossible angles the boat twisted through as she threatened to capsize.

That's when I learned that fear isn't so bad after all. Of course, at times we need to listen to our fears and flee as fast as we can from danger. For so many of the girls I've met who have been trafficked, the inability to escape danger has been a uniquely horrible torture. But for me, being scared wasn't the worst thing that could happen. In fact, it changed my life for the better.

So often I hid from difficult situations, distracting myself with a manic burst of activity at the gym. But even though I was burning about eight thousand calories a day on the ocean, I had to face the waves and the dark and agonizing ache of missing my wonderful mum—perhaps for the first time in my life. And I'm so glad that I did.

"I'm never doing *this* again. Ever." I must have said that many times during the row, and I meant it every time. But I'd get out there in a heartbeat if there was a chance that doing it might help the fight against human trafficking. Besides, in many ways, I miss it. I miss the feeling of being small and invisible out there. I miss the sense of having everything I needed in that little cabin. Life was simpler then, and I've grown wise about some ways in which modern living complicates life despite claims to simplify it.

The row made an impact on every aspect of my life, even the parts that I'd never have thought would be affected. Money is one example. I always wore heels, and the thought of going out wearing flats and no makeup would have horrified me. I wore so much makeup that one day a friend came up to me with a kind look in her eyes and asked whether the red mark on my cheek was a bruise. I said that it was, but I was just too embarrassed to admit that I'd gotten carried away with the blusher that morning. I must have spent almost $10,000 on nails alone from the time when I was eighteen until I broke up with Ben. All the time I was with Fazil I was buying things I couldn't afford with credit cards. My debts increased, and I slipped into denial.

I arrived in Barbados as a woman who knew herself for the first time. These days everything's so different from the way it was before the row. I'm more interested in sports bras and a good pair of running shoes than heels and handbags, and I feel much happier in myself. I feel that I have grown up. I used to wear bright colors and major brands so that I would be noticed and accepted. But not now. These days less is more. I don't feel that I have to try so hard to please people.

I've learned to admit when I mess up. I'm not so scared of people disliking me, so I'm free to say I'm sorry. I thought I knew who I was before this whole adventure began, but somewhere between seeing Mum slip away from me and feeling the fear and exhaustion on the boat, I learned that I had no clue about who I was. I found someone different within me.

Who would I be right now if I'd never seen that movie and gotten stirred up by the horrors of trafficking? I don't know for sure, but I do know that I would have missed out on feeling passionate, sad, angry, and full of purpose as I have been. The old Julia would have run a mile from feeling such complicated, difficult emotions, but not anymore. Now I want more of them. Now I want to be disturbed and propelled by the compassion to act. It's like the Polish poet Cyprian Norwid said: "To be what is called happy; one should have (1) something to live on, (2) something to live for, and (3) something to die for. The lack of one of these results in drama. The lack of two results in tragedy."[2]

I don't want my life to be a tragedy of emptiness. I want it to be full. I want it to count. I guess that's why I took up cycling not long after I got back. I'd never done much of it before, not properly at least. But it has taught me plenty. I've learned on team rides that the leader takes the hit of the strong winds. The front rider shelters the team and protects them, helping them ride more efficiently. It's helped to learn this and see that it's right to expect leadership to be tough and emotionally draining. And just as it is on the bike, there are times to slip back into the pack and let someone else take the lead for a while.

I've thought so much about trafficking. What we did was so small compared to the scale of the problem, but it's clearer than ever that—like Mother Teresa said—we can "do small things with great love."[3] Not that it compares to the pain of the thirty million, but I loved feeling the pain of the row. And that love felt as though it was an overflow of the love I'd received from God. Each stroke of the oar was a small act, but a lot of love was in each one. If you and I and your friends and mine did a whole load of small acts, we'd start to make a real impact on the problem of human trafficking.

Something grabbed me. It wasn't as if I was brought up in a household of social activists, and even as I started to carve out a life for myself, I was never that interested in charitable organizations or causes. I can only conclude that something grabbed me, shook me up, and left me totally disturbed. Something wouldn't let me rest until I started to do something about it. That sounds exactly like the kind of thing that God would do. The Bible is full of stories that are like mine: everyday screwups being prodded by God and given a job to do. A few of those stories—like those of Moses, Joshua, and Jonah—involve crossing water too.

On the second day of the row, when the battery tester failed, Kate turned to me and said, "Nothing else will go wrong, will it, Julia?"

"No way!" I said. "Nothing else is going to break, fail, or snap." I believed with all my heart that God had us and that we were going to be okay.

And then, every one of the fourteen days that followed, we watched as something went wrong.

My naivety was helpful. Had I known what pain and struggle awaited us on the ocean I'm not at all sure that I would have signed up for the row. But believing that it was going to be fine, having blind faith and wide-eyed optimism, prevented me from being scared off. We have been taught to frown on being naive, inexperienced, and ill-equipped for the job, but I wonder whether we miss out on great adventures if we listen too carefully to the warnings. Sometimes, we have to take a risk. That's what faith is all about: taking a risk that God is real, that my actions here on earth count, and that my failings and mistakes don't define me but cause me to grow and learn.

What I did wasn't anything new, and it wasn't all that remarkable. We broke two world records, but masses of people risk far more than we did to change the lives of people who have been trafficked. They're the people who stop the boat, jump in, and grab the bottle. They're the ones who choose to do something difficult and unexpected, facing the very real risk of failure. But they keep going anyway.

All of us can't row an ocean, but all of us can do something. And doing something starts by opening our eyes to the world around us and looking out for something that needs to change. It means allowing ourselves to feel disturbed, not running away from fear, and choosing not to distract ourselves with life as usual when the going gets tough. It means jumping into the water and grabbing the bottle. It means doing something because something will change the world.

Epilogue

It's funny, but it turns out that if you really, really want to learn more about yourself, and if you really, really want to discover just how strong is your inner resolve and how fragile is your ego, then you should definitely row an ocean. Forget all that stuff about how strong your legs will get, how good you'll become at celestial navigation, or how skillful you'll be at pooing in a bucket in the middle of a gale. Yes, you'll come home with all those wonderful things added to your résumé, but believe me, it's the inner lessons that sink in the deepest. In time the calluses heal and the muscle cramps wear off, but the changes to your character will stay with you far longer.

I often describe the row as the hardest but the best thing I've ever done. At the toughest points on the ocean, life became a simple matter of getting out of the cabin and pulling the oars for 120 minutes. As long as I could do that, I'd get through it.

And now, back on land and two years after the row ended, I'm still putting that lesson into practice, especially when things don't go as I hope they would. With any setback, any disappointment, anything that doesn't work out in the way I'd imagined it would—as well as the many more things that go brilliantly and far exceed my expectations—I remind myself to get back on the oars and do that one essential thing that I know I'm meant to be focusing on right now. I tell myself to focus on what I can do, not worry about what I can't.

As I write this, the world is mourning the passing of Nelson Mandela. So many times over the last few days I've stopped and stared at the quote that automatically appears at the end of every e-mail I send, wise words from the man himself: "Sport has the power to change the world. It has the power to inspire. It has the power to unite people, in a way that little else does. It speaks to youth in a language they understand. Sport can create hope where once there was only despair. It is more powerful than governments in breaking down racial barriers."[1]

If ever there was a man who knew about change, it was Mandela. He understood that our defeats are just as important as our victories. He knew that if we want to see transformation, we need to persevere through whatever difficulties are in front of us.

These days I don't call people *victims* of human trafficking. Instead I call them *survivors*. So many of the survivors that I have met are doing well and are rebuilding strong, healthy lives. They aren't victims anymore. Mandela knew that too. He could have given in to resentment or fear and chosen to flee or hide from view. Yet he didn't. He reached out. He chose to learn from the hard stuff, not hide from it.

I've had to draw deep on this a lot lately. In the last year, I've set up Sport for Freedom as a charity, and it has taken plenty of resolve and focus. We have just started in a UK safehouse to rehabilitate survivors of trafficking through sport and adventure. We are pioneering a model that we can use nationwide and globally.

Because we know that prevention is better than cure, we are using sport as an educational, preventative tool among some of the most vulnerable, roughest, and poorest communities in the UK. My hope is that as more people join in the fight against human trafficking, charities such as Sport for Freedom will one day cease to exist. Wouldn't it be great if there were no need for us because modern day slavery had been abolished?

Admittedly, that's a pretty big dream, but isn't that how all the best adventures start out: with excitement about the idea of reaching the other side, even if the route across seems a little daunting at first?

We are all leaders. Whenever we come into contact with others, we have the power to influence their lives, the potential to inspire them, to make them think, and to reconsider things.

We don't always feel that way, though. Too often we feel as though we're rushing too far too fast, not really making enough of an impact in any of our situations. Too often, we spread ourselves too thin. We sign up for more updates than we can read and get excited about more causes than we can really help. These days I'm wondering whether instead of giving badly to ten things and spreading ourselves thinly, we'd all be better off just giving well to a few things.

No matter how ordinary your background, how messy your past, or how limited your experience, the extraordinary is not beyond you. It is out there, waiting for you to tackle it, bit by bit. Whatever it is—a half marathon or a polar trek, a hidden dream that got buried long ago, or a wild-eyed adventure that you've never thought possible but secretly hoped it might be—the way to the finish line is ahead of you. Take the first of a million small steps today, and your journey has already begun.

Five Things You Can Do to Fight Human Trafficking

1. LOOK AT YOUR HANDS

Each of us has skills and opportunities that can be put to use to help the fight against trafficking. Whether you love sport, music, fashion, baking, or painting, anything you're passionate about can be used for freedom.

We have supporters using their hobbies and skills to raise money for us, and others who have chosen to give us a percentage of their business profits. Whatever you do, you can do it to help others.

Would you pray for us too? We need all the prayers we can get!

2. LOOK AT YOUR SHOPPING

If something's really cheap, the chances are that somewhere along the line a worker wasn't paid properly, if at all. Slave labor stretches all the way to our favorite shopping malls, despite the fact that it is so well hidden. Take a look at slaveryfootprint.org to find out how your shopping habits make an impact.

It's really important that we learn how to ask questions about the lives of those who were involved in the preparation of the items we buy. Buying goods that carry the Fair Trade logo is a great way to start, as it ensures that those involved in the production were paid a fair wage and employed in good conditions. Have a look at fairtradeusa.org to find out more.

You can also donate regularly to Sport for Freedom. Monthly giving makes a huge difference in our ability to grow sustainably and change many lives for the better.

3. LOOK AT YOUR TV

Get your friends thinking—and then talking—about the realities of human trafficking by hosting a movie night. Films like *Taken, Human Trafficking,* or *The Whistle Blower* will get a good discussion going. And if you want to raise some money, you could collect donations and sell snacks, with the proceeds being given away to help the fight against trafficking.

Once you've gotten people interested, why not tell them about Sport for Freedom and see if they want to get involved with one of our campaigns?

4. LOOK AT YOUR COMPUTER

When it comes to the fight against modern-day slavery, the Internet has a lot to offer—and a lot to answer for. It's a brilliant educational tool for reading and researching. Use your social media reach to tell others what you've learned. And once you've educated yourself, host an event—whether it's in your school, college, church group, Scouts, or corporation—where you can educate, inform, and inspire others.

The dark side of the Internet is that certain aspects of it fuel trafficking. Even though many people don't link pornography with human trafficking, the truth is that by viewing porn, users are adding to the demand. And where criminals see a way of making money out of selling sex, they'll not hesitate to force people to take part against their will. If you know people who look at porn (or strip clubs for that matter) as harmless, challenge them.

One more thing: it would be great if you could follow Sport for Freedom on Facebook, Twitter, and Instagram! We'd love to hear what you're doing for freedom.

Visit us at *sportforfreedom.org*
Facebook: *facebook.com/SportforFreedom*
Twitter: @SPORTforFREEDOM and #ForFREEDOM
Instagram: instagram.com/sportforfreedom

5. LOOK AT YOUR LEADERS

Write to your political representatives and request to meet with them. Ask them to do all they can to raise the profile of the fight against human trafficking. Get your friends and fellow voters (or future voters if they're young!) to join in. Use your social media reach to demonstrate that you're serious about the cause, and make sure you give your representatives lots of public praise whenever they do speak out and use their influence.

Acknowledgments

It's hard to know where to start, but firstly I'd like to thank my precious mummy. Thank you for being an absolute inspiration and example of kindness, gentleness, and strength. You are a woman of few words. You let your life do the talking and have walked the narrow road with integrity, passion, and tenacity. Your adventurous spirit, persevering zeal, and solid faith have enabled me to finally start becoming the woman I want to be.

Isi, thank you for blessing me to share our family story. It takes courage to be able to support your daughter as she shares the tough times so that others may be encouraged and strengthened. Thank you for all your practical help always, no matter the hour. Your passions for sport, cars, and geography have too become my passions. Thank you for giving me the most precious gift of all—my relationship with Jesus Christ.

Joy—aka Sissy—Mum and Dad named you perfectly: you are the joy in my life. Thank you for holding my hand in my darkest valleys and laughing with me in my happiest times. You are the most selfless and generous person I know. You give and you give some more. Your sacrifice and humility overwhelm me. Words simply aren't enough. I love you. Thank you for blessing me with the most wonderful niece and nephew.

Thank you to my extended family: Ewen, I love you with all my heart. Noel, Maureen, Lorraine, Niamh, and Erin, we have been through a lot but laughed all the more.

Craig Borlase: There wouldn't be a book if it wasn't for you. When we met you just "got it." We clicked instantly, and it has been an utter joy to work together. You listened to hours upon hours of my story and have captured it in a way that I believe nobody else could have. You are talented beyond belief, and I'm delighted to have gained a friend in you.

Don Jacobson: I never imagined an ordinary girl from Slough would end up publishing a book. You saw the potential and made it a reality. Your brainstorming, wisdom, and prayers have meant so much to me. Marty Raz and Blair Jacobson at DCJA, thank you for being so efficient and helpful always.

Matt Baugher and the Thomas Nelson team: Thank you for publishing my story and for being such fun to work with. To the best editors ever, Meaghan Porter and Paula Major: I am so grateful for your hard work, dedication, and attention to detail. You have made this publishing journey so enjoyable.

Stephanie and Joe Thompson: Who'd have thought rowing the Atlantic would bring forth so many adventures on and off the water? This all started with you, Stephanie. Thank you for being my best friend and blessing me to fulfill what was our dream. I know we will tackle an adventure together soon.

Chrissie Abbott: *Thank you* doesn't even come close. Thank you for believing in me and in the row when I doubted and wavered. Thanks for encouraging me and praying with me every Monday evening. You love me unconditionally. You are my rock. I love you dearly.

Jane Overnell: You have shown me love in a whole new way. Your example is like treasure and causes me to want to grow and learn. Thank you for carrying me up the mountains of life when I'm scared, praying with me, and making me laugh 'til my sides hurt.

Nicky and Pippa Gumbel: I've never seen such grace and humility modeled as I do in you. Your leadership is authentic, and you have taught me more than you will ever know by your example. Thank you for pioneering Alpha: it changed my life and bought me back to my relationship with God. Thank you to all my HTB Church family; there are too many to thank personally, but your friendship and community cause me to be continually challenged and inspired. I love doing life with you Monday to Saturday. Sunday is the icing on a rich cake!

Matt and Beth Redman: Your kindness is holiness. Thank you for your friendship and love. Beth, you are my sword sissy.

J. John and Killy; Cathy and Gary Clarke; Bobbie and Brian Houston; Christine and Nick Caine; Louie and Shelley Giglio; and Lisa and John Bevere: Your example and leadership from near and far have influenced me throughout my life—thank you. Chris, I'm so grateful to you and the A21 Campaign for awakening me and so many globally to this injustice of human trafficking. Thank you to both A21 and ECPAT UK for all your support to our campaign and us as a crew.

Andy Cairns and Julie Featherstone: Thank you for allowing me to pursue my dream. I know you thought I was crazy, but you supported me all the same. A special thanks also to Anna Edwards. I love my job and our Sky Sports News team; it's a pleasure to work with the best in the business and with so many friends.

Bear Grylls: Thank you for being such an inspiration in my life. You are gutsy, vulnerable, and so kind. Thank you for encouraging me with the row and for all your support. I wouldn't have wanted anyone else to write the foreword for this book.

Sir Matthew Pinsent: Thank you for being so generous with your time and helping us with our training and our campaign. You are one of life's genuine, good guys. You are fun, giving, and so humble. Thank you for your practical support and encouragement.

Toby Garbett and David Kingston: Thank you for teaching me to row! The endless hours of correcting and tweaking gave me the confidence to row the Atlantic. I am forever grateful to you.

The number and quality of friends I have made along the way during this adventure are mind-blowing. James Ketchell and Margaret Bowling: You are seasoned adventurers and Atlantic rowers, and I will forever be indebted to your encouragement and practical help. Dave and Yvette Kershaw: We connected through the cause, but your practical help and physio when my hamstrings were in continual pain was such a blessing. Thank you to Complete Physiotherapy, for sponsoring me, and also James Drabble, my personal trainer.

Thank you to all our sponsors for enabling us to get to the start line and make this crossing for freedom. It has been a pleasure to work with you and gain so many friends in you. Thank you to Captive Minds, our PR team.

A special thanks to David and Sylvia Andrews and Stuart Marvin, David Arkless, Conny Czymoch, and Sarah Summers for your belief and investment in me in so many ways.

Deborah Paul: thank you for being there for me during my darkest moment on the ocean. Laura Drew: I'll never forget spotting you first in Barbados, screaming with the largest Finnish flag. Ali Gillum and Tim Matthews: thanks for continually encouraging me to write this book. Thank you to Louis Greig, Bronwynn Joyce, Sundeep Chohan, Natasha Finch, Ugo Monye, Melinda and

Simon Reading, Lavinia Brennan, Marika Brennan, Dee Watts, Al and Liv Gordon, Andrew Wallis, Rosie Orozco, and the Richards family for your continual support.

Thank you to all my friends near and far, for cheering me on and supporting me so much and to all those around the world who followed and encouraged us too. You'll never know how much that meant.

To the most incredible Sport for Freedom team who enable us to bring freedom through our work: Thank you for your passion, "whatever it takes" attitude, and relentless determination.

Katie, Kate, Debs and Helen: There wouldn't be a book at all had it not been for you. Thank you for saying yes to the most extraordinary challenge. It wouldn't have been possible without each and every one of our commitments, relentless work, and passion. I have never been stretched to such limits physically and mentally, and I couldn't have and wouldn't have wanted to do it without you. When almost everything failed, we had and found everything in each other. I am eternally grateful to you.

"When you pass through the waters, I will be with you" (Isaiah 43:2 NKJV). Thank you, God, for your promise then and now on this adventure of life . . . .

Julia Immonen
London, February 2014

———

I am grateful to Michael O'Neill at Stewardship for taking the trouble to put Julia and me in touch back in 2012. Thanks are also due to Matt and Beth for putting in a good word, and Martin and Emily for helping me see the potential within Julia's story.

As is so often the case, my eyes were far too small to see this book's true potential, and it took my friend and agent, Don Jacobson, to open them up. I am so grateful for all those three-way Skypes where we dreamed, laughed, and prayed together.

Bear Grylls was exceptionally kind, and Julia's family was exceptionally brave. Kate Richardson helped me to understand the story in a new way, and Stephanie Thompson gave great feedback on the manuscript. Sophie Hayes's book *Trafficked* was compelling, disturbing, and helpful in so many ways, and Emily Vesey helped bring human trafficking into focus.

Marty Raz and Blair Jacobson at DCJA went above and beyond yet again to make sure that we got published (and paid!). As ever, I owe you more thanks than this little paragraph will allow.

I am indebted to Matt Baugher and the whole team at Thomas Nelson, especially our editor-par-excellence Meaghan Porter, who has redefined every one of my assumptions about what an editor can do and impart. And Dimples Kellogg has used her skill to help to make this a far better book.

This book was written with the album *Kveikur* on constant repeat and would not have been possible without Emma, Evie, Barney, Bess, and LibLob Borlase being happy for me to miss out on Wales for a few days while I found Julia's voice.

Finally, thank you, Julia, for trusting me with your story. It has been a joy and a pleasure. Long may you continue to live for freedom.

Craig Borlase
Compton, February 2014

Notes

Chapter 3: Broken

1. For more information about the Alpha course, visit alpha
.org or alphausa.org.

Chapter 4: Deciding to Row an Ocean

1. The A21 Campaign, *The Problem*, booklet, 2;
http://neutrinodata.s3.amazonaws.com/a21/userimages
/The Problem.pdf.
2. *Profits and Poverty: The Economics of Forced Labour*,
International Labour Office (Geneva, 2014), 13; www.ilo
.org/wcmsp5/groups/public/---ed_norm/---declaration
/documents/publication/wcms_243391.pdf.
3. Carina Kolodny, "Slavery Is Still Thriving and Is More
Profitable Than Big Oil," *Huffington Post*, May 22, 2014,
www.huffingtonpost.com/2014/05/22/modern-slavery
-profits-big-oil_n_5365220.html.
4. "Sex Trade, Forced Labor Top U.N. Human Trafficking
List," February 16, 2009, CNN.com, www.cnn
.com/2009/WORLD/asiapcf/02/16/un.trafficking/.

5. "11 Facts About Human Trafficking,"
   DoSomething.org, http://www.dosomething.org
   /tiposandtools/11-facts-about-human-trafficking#.
6. John W. Whitehead, "Sex Trafficking: There's More to
   the Super Bowl than Sports," *Huffington Post*, February 6,
   2011, www.huffingtonpost.com/john-w-whitehead
   /sex-trafficking-super-bowl_b_816618.html.
7. Michael Curtis, "Slavery in the World Today," *American
   Thinker*, October 25, 2013, www.americanthinker.com
   /2013/10/slavery_in_the_world_today.html. The figure
   comes from the Global Slavery Index 2013.
8. The A21 Campaign, *The Problem.*

Chapter 13: Stories in the Waters

1. David W. Shaw, *Daring the Sea* (New York: Kensington
   Publishing, 2003), 30–33.
2. Ibid., 39, 50, 69, 214.
3. Joe Segura, "Shore Patrol: LB Rower Sets Course for
   Record Crossing," *Press-Telegram*, December 10, 2008,
   www.presstelegram.com/technology/20081211
   /shore-patrol-lb-rower-sets-course-for-record-crossing.
4. Marie-Therese and Bengt Danielsson, "Tales of Great
   Pacific Rowers," *Pacific Islands Monthly*, April 1983,
   www.oceanrowing.com/anders_svedlund/press/tales
   _of_%20great.htm.
5. Ibid.
6. Ibid.
7. "Rowers Lost at Sea," Ocean Rowing Society, www
   .oceanrowing.com/statistics/lost_at_sea.htm.

8. Tom McCann, "Dr. Nenad Belic, 62," *Chicago Tribune News*, December 10, 2001, articles.chicagotribune .com/2001-12-10/news/0112100002_1_adventurous-spirit-trip-storm; Peggy Wolff, "Nenad Belic, Taken by Storm," Chicagomag.com, February 25, 2002, www.oceanrowing .com/logs/Nenad_Belic.htm. The paragraphs about Belic rely on Wolff's story cited here.

Chapter 16: Rope and Glue

1. Ship size: Maritime Connector, www.maritime-connector .comi/wiki/chinamax/; Speed: John Vidal, "Modern Cargo Ships Slow to the Speed of the Sailing Clippers," *Observer*, July 24, 2010, www.theguardian.com/environment /2010/jul/25/slow-ships-cut-greenhouse-emissions; Conversion of knots to miles per hour: www.convertunits.com/from/mph/to/knots.
2. "Containers Overboard," Vero Marine Insurance, www.veromarine.co.nz/dirvz/marine/marine.nsf/Content /PhotoFeature0007.

Chapter 17: Prayers to Michael

1. David W. Shaw, *Daring the Sea* (New York: Kensington Publishing, 2003).

Chapter 19: Something to Row For

1. Michael Curtis, "Slavery in the World Today," *American Thinker*, October 25, 2013, www.americanthinker.com /2013/10/slavery_in_the_world_today.html. The figure comes from the Global Slavery Index 2013.
2. Amanda Walker-Rodriguez and Rodney Hill, "Human Sex Trafficking," *FBI Law Enforcement Bulletin*, March 2011, www.fbi.gov/stats-services/publications/law -enforcement-bulletin/march_2011/human_sex_trafficking.

3. "The Truth of the Matter," Rescueher.org, www.rescueher .org/facts

Chapter 28: The Missed Bottle

1. Philippians 4:13 (NKJV); Isaiah 43:2 (NKJV); Galatians 6:9 (NIV).
2. Cyprian Norwid quoted in *The Oxford Handbook of Happiness*, Susan David, Ilona Boniwell, Amanda Conly Ayers, eds. (Oxford University Press, 2013), 98.
3. Cited in Brian Kolodiejchuk, ed., *Mother Teresa: Come Be My Light* (New York: Random House, 2007), 34.

Epilogue

1. Nelson Mandela, address at Laureus World Sports Awards, 2000, http://www.youtube.com/watch?v=-9awPf5SJ1E.

About the Authors

J ULIA IMMONEN was born and raised in Finland before her family moved to the UK when she was six. One of her passions is campaigning to end modern-day slavery. An avid sportswoman who works for Sky Sports News, Julia is the founder of Sport for Freedom, an anti-human trafficking charity based in London. She is an international motivational speaker who uses her passion and story to inspire others. Follow Julia's adventures on Twitter@ JuliaImmonen and Instagram: JuliaKImmonen.

C RAIG BORLASE is an author and collaborative writer living in England. With more than thirty books to his credit— some written in collaboration with other authors—Craig is more fascinated than ever by the power of a real-life story to inspire and transform a reader. He is married with four young children.

DREAM IT.
DO IT.
END IT.

SWIM. CYCLE. RUN.
CLIMB. SAIL. RIDE. BOX.
SKI. SURF. SKYDIVE.

**What will you do
#ForFREEDOM?**

Sport
for Freedom
uses the
positive power
of community
and sport to bring
freedom from human
trafficking and modern-
day slavery.

Our mission is threefold:

ACTION: we use sporting challenges
locally and globally to raise awareness,
educate, and inspire others to action.

EDUCATION: we use sport as a preventive,
educational tool among some of the most
vulnerable communities in the UK.

REHABILITATION: we use sport, fitness, and
adventure to rehabilitate and reintegrate survivors
of human trafficking back into society.

SPORT
FOR FREEDOM

Follow us:

www.SportforFreedom.org